You Already Know

You Already Know

The Science of Mastering Your Intuition

Laura Huang

PORTFOLIO | PENGUIN

Portfolio / Penguin
An imprint of Penguin Random House LLC
1745 Broadway, New York, NY 10019
penguinrandomhouse.com

Most Portfolio books are available at a discount when purchased in quantity for sales promotions or corporate use. Special editions, which include personalized covers, excerpts, and corporate imprints, can be created when purchased in large quantities. For more information, please call (212) 572-2232 or e-mail specialmarkets@penguinrandomhouse.com. Your local bookstore can also assist with discounted bulk purchases using the Penguin Random House corporate Business-to-Business program. For assistance in locating a participating retailer, e-mail B2B@penguinrandomhouse.com.

PORTFOLIO and PORTFOLIO with javelin thrower design
are registered trademarks of Penguin Random House LLC.

The following photographs and artwork are courtesy of artist Amanda Phingbodhipakkiya: Atlantic Avenue-Barclays Center Subway Station, New York City on page 172; Public Billboard, New York City on page 172; *We Are Tomorrow* (2022) at the US Embassy, Bangkok, Thailand on page 173, and photograph of U.S. Ambassador to Thailand Robert F. Godec and Amanda Phingbodhipakkiya by Matt Hunt on page 174.

Diagram on page 112 used with permission of Dr. Haibin Liu. Diagram on page 118 used with permission of Dr. Bradley Peterson.

BOOK DESIGN BY ALISSA ROSE THEODOR

Library of Congress record available at https://lccn.loc.gov/2024053786

ISBN 9780593714768 (hardcover)
ISBN 9780593714775 (ebook)

Printed in the United States of America
1st Printing

The authorized representative in the EU for product safety and compliance is Penguin Random House Ireland, Morrison Chambers, 32 Nassau Street, Dublin D02 YH68, Ireland, https://eu-contact.penguin.ie.

For Baba, who taught me to listen to what whispers and not what screams

Contents

Preface

I was picking up my teenage son from basketball practice and watched the last few minutes. His coach, DeShawn, was doing a drill where he set the boys up two-on-two. Two boys on offense trying to score; two boys on defense trying to prevent them from scoring. The boys on offense were told that they were allowed six passes, and then they had a single opportunity to shoot and score. If they scored, they got a point; if they didn't score, they switched to defense and the other team got the ball. The other team would then get six passes and an opportunity to score.

I watched with casual interest. My eyes shot open, however, when DeShawn started shouting at the boys midway through the drill: "*Why* do you think I gave you *six passes*? Why are you shooting after just *one* or *two* passes?"

He paused, realized that none of the boys had an answer, and then continued, "Look, the first *one* or *two* passes, you, everyone is just going on raw motions and guesses and getting a sense for the experience of defending these guys." He went on, "The *third* and the *fourth* passes, that's when you're starting to notice things, like the way your defender moves to a certain side and catches you off guard, or how he angles his body a certain way to fake you out, or tends toward a certain style of defense, or positions his feet facing the basket or not, or the way they support and flank each other or not. You're starting to pick up on their patterns and yours!"

My ears really perked up at this point.

"By the *fifth* or *sixth* pass, now you know them. You got them. You got what they're doing, what their deal is, where they have weaknesses. You're ready to predict, to act, and to shoot. And it's *going* to go in."

That's what this book is about. You've already experienced the first two passes. It encompasses your background; what you've learned, absorbed, and accumulated over time; and everything you've lived through. You have the experience, the exposure.

We're going to start noticing things in the third and fourth passes—recognizing, diagnosing, and interpreting the information and data that is whispering to us, as well as regulating, mediating, and tempering the erroneous information that is screaming at us— so that by the fifth and sixth passes, we can intentionally activate our intuition and take action. We're going to activate it, predict it, act on it, and shoot. And it's going to go in.

Introduction

In 2008, I began work on my PhD dissertation, which was titled *A Theory of Investor Gut Feel: A Test of the Impact of Gut Feel on Entrepreneurial Investment Decisions*. I was curious about how investors (really) decide what start-ups to fund. Is it actually about the financials, the business model, the metrics, the hard data? Or, as I suspected, do they just use their gut feel? What is their gut feel comprised of? Did the hard data reinforce their gut feel or interfere with it? How did their prior experience influence it? Gut feel was thought to be inexplicable and unquantifiable. Could I *quantify the unquantifiable*?

I was told by dozens of esteemed scholars not to study this topic. It's a slang term, they said. It's an atheoretical* line of questioning, they said. It's a paradox that can't be answered, they said. You'll never get a job; you'll never publish this work, they said.

---

* The academic equivalent of the worst insult you could sling at someone, being atheoretical means that your work has no theoretical basis and is not founded on anything real.

I decided to study it anyway.

My wonderfully supportive advisor was the one notable exception to this group of naysayers. She told me these were worthy questions to pursue, and that if they were questions that I really wanted to study and answer, then haters be damned. "Why even get a PhD if not to study a question that you really want to discover the answer to?" she said. (She had a gut feel, she later told me.)

I began by interviewing investors on how they make their investment decisions. For a long time, I didn't mention the term *gut feel* at all, partly because I was still twice bitten and multiple times shy, but mainly because I wanted to see if they would use or allude to the term without my prompting. Even I didn't expect every single investor to gloss over the "hard" data—information in the form of financials, business models, and any sort of analysis in written form—so quickly and so fluidly and discuss how their gut feel drove their decisions.

That opened up different types of questions: When did they invest in a start-up because they *just had a feeling*, even when all the hard data told them that it looked like a bad deal on paper? When did they choose not to invest in a particular start-up because they had sneaking suspicions, even when all the hard data pointed to a unicorn?

The interviews led to inductive theories, which developed into grounded theories, which were tested in field experiments and longitudinal field studies. Translation: I did a ton of work,* and my husband would wake up to hear me muttering about gut feel in my sleep for years.

---

* The full dissertation, including all the methodology, can be accessed by the link noted in the first endnote. I won't be offended by anyone who doesn't take me up on this.

When I completed the dissertation in 2012,* there were a few significant findings that jumped out at me. First, investor gut feel was *experience-based*. It was uniquely personal and individual and could not be replicated or passed down from person to person. Which meant something important: Once these investors tried to *explain* their gut feel to someone else—to justify the logic underlying it—they would essentially talk themselves out of the right decision. Being able to intuit is a skill, built up over years of personal experience.

But second, it was informed by data and analytical information. The rich interaction between personal experience and external data produced an outcome: Gut feel was actually the *impulse* at the end of this *process*, which was based on both *thinking and feeling*. Rather than being based on rapid, nonconscious compulsion, as much of prior literature suggested, what investors called their "gut feel" was the final result of an elaborate "intuiting process" that was rooted in dynamic, expertise-based emotion-cognitions—experience *and* data—specific to the entrepreneurship context. In other words, data was certainly a factor in the intuiting process, but by the time they had a gut feel, the data had already been so neatly folded into their emotional experiences that it no longer appeared to be *just* data, or even neutral information. Instead, it helped them make sense of and was claimed as personal reflections. Much like drinking an enjoyable iced tea on a hot day, we understand that there were once solid granules of sugar dissolved in water, but we just enjoy the refreshing liquid beverage as a whole.

It's here where I answered a question that had been nagging at me for some time: Is there a difference between intuition and gut feel?

---

* The average amount of time to complete a PhD is five to seven years. Five to seven looong years, which often make you feel like it was fifteen to seventeen years.

The answer is a resounding yes. Intuition is the process that leads to a final moment of recognition that we call our gut feel. The process and the outcome are distinct.* Granted, the process may last mere seconds (or, alternatively, drag on for years). We might be consciously aware that we're in the midst of that process or not. Either way, there *is* a moment at which we just *know*. Oftentimes while looking back, we describe this moment with the following words: "I just had a gut feel. I just knew."

The third significant finding from my dissertation research was that individuals who trusted *this* gut feel (the outcome of their intuiting process), rather than an arbitrary thought while still in the midst of the intuiting process, found that it doesn't lie.

Let me explain this a bit more, because at first glance, it might seem ridiculous. There is no part of our brain that is 100 percent right 100 percent of the time—not your reasoning, not your memory, not your gut feel. The idea that you can trust your gut feel all the time is as misguided as the idea that you can trust that the data reported is always solid and untainted.

It's situational. Gut feel is fully and absolutely effective in the right contexts—inadequate, even damaging, in the wrong ones. Gut feel is not for *every* decision. Investors who relied on their gut feel for complex and chaotic decisions—contexts in which they had

---

* Some might say: But isn't this just a question of semantics? Couldn't one argue that intuition is also the end result of the intuiting process? In which case, intuition and gut feel would be synonymous? After all, *intuition* and *gut feel* are terms often used interchangeably in both research studies and everyday conversation. Both are part of our verbiage and nomenclature: *The psychology of intuition* is often referred to in the science of judgment and decision-making, whereas its practical application is expressed as *trusting your gut feel*. I argue that intuition is the process and gut feel is the outcome, and the two are distinct. Until we understand the full process, we can never understand what the right outcome should look like. By delineating between *intuition* and *gut feel*, *you'll* know better, and knowing the difference will lead you to breakthroughs that you never thought possible.

to rely on their gut feel because it was the (only) way for them to manage the complexity and extreme risk associated with the decision to invest money into certain start-ups—found that their gut feel was spot-on. Take Uber, for example. When Uber was in its infancy, it screamed "bad investment": The company faced regulatory challenges fraught with legal battles and airport bans; they had technology risks and glitches in their mobile app, including algorithmic pricing that often shut down operations; they had no established market position; and not to mention, there were all the implied and underlying feelings about the business itself. *(This is terrifying. Why would I or anyone voluntarily get into a stranger's personal car?)*

Yet, despite these challenges, investors had a gut feel. It was a gut feel that emboldened them to trust their prior experience and their own inner voices and make an investment that would otherwise be considered overly risky and likely to lead to failure. In academic speak: Their gut feel allowed them to cognitively and emotionally reframe investment risk into a compelling narrative that transcended avoidance behavior and led them to invest. Put simply: A small set of investors saw that they weren't betting on Uber as much as they were betting that the taxi industry was broken and that there were major changes and disruption that would be coming to the public transportation industry.

This type of decision-making is quiet *and* intentional. It is informed by both the data that we have and the experience that we've accumulated and results in a personal, internal signal that is straining to be heard. Distinguishing between this kind of signal on the one hand and wishful thinking and what others are saying—social conversations, people's expectations, the media, bandwagons, etc.—on the other is hard because the latter speaks much louder. These forces are also much more unrelenting; there are even modern-day algorithms that target you until you're forced to listen. We can't help but notice what is louder, brasher, more flamboyant. But we can also learn and train ourselves to listen to what whispers, not what screams.

And finally, fourth, almost by corollary, what jumped out to me was that the power of intuition was not *just* about making the "right decision"; it was also about the ability to take *quick action* on that gut feel at the right time. The fact that gut feel is quiet often prevents us from being able to take intentional and quick action. Decisiveness.

Quick action is part of what makes a decision the "right decision." It's true that investors never have the counterfactual, the alternate ending had they taken a different course of action. But making a choice and making it work—sometimes by fixing or overhauling it or course-correcting—actually made it *the* right investment. It was a virtuous cycle where that decision led to their ability to mentor, make introductions, provide resources and know-how, get access to increasingly better deals and sort through them, and continue to use their gut feel to take future action—all more effectively. And they achieved extremely high levels of success as a result.

Gaining an Edge by Relying on Your Gut Feel

We call lots of things gut feel. Gut feel is not just emotion. It is not just information. Gut feel is the result of data plus experience, colliding and combining to create a remarkable reaction, not unlike the nuclear reaction that occurs when atoms collide. All of the most successful investors had learned and understood this. They also had learned to develop, harness, and activate their gut feel. But what about everyone else, I wondered?

So, post-2012, post-dissertation, I expanded my research to include leaders, managers, organizers, trailblazers, seekers, and aspirers to test whether my hypothesis—that the most successful people in the world (outside of investors) are those who have learned how to develop, harness, and activate their gut feel—would hold.

I interviewed thousands of individuals in the workforce, asking them how they define success, trying to figure out what made (makes) them successful and whether they would mention gut feel. Were there certain qualities that they shared, clusters of characteristics that were indicative of those who were "successful" versus those who fell short?

I interviewed those who have achieved both traditional definitions of success (Olympic athletes, world-record holders, Pulitzer Prize winners, CEOs of companies, entrepreneurs who have taken their companies public), as well as those who might be considered nontraditional successes (formerly incarcerated individuals who have gotten back on their feet; women successfully returning to the workforce after leaving for decades to raise their children; rock stars making comebacks after major accidents, addictions, and trauma).

The first factor every single person credited was hard work. What was intriguing, however, was that the more I dug under the surface, the more I found that they each seemed to believe, deep down, that hard work was a bit of a farce. Hard work was the "right," expected answer. What they actually believed was that even though hard work is critical, hard work alone is not enough. You can take two different people who work equally as hard, and one will inevitably be much more successful than the other. Why is that? The truly successful ones figured out what gave them an edge. They could take signals, perceptions, cues, and even stereotypes and flip them in their favor to create an advantage. This was the equivalent of taking their hard work, and making it work harder for them. Based on that research and those findings, I wrote my first book, *Edge: Turning Adversity into Advantage*.

This book, my second, is about the (only) other factor that 100 percent of the successful people interviewed mentioned: gut feel. But their descriptions weren't straightforward. Some gave their gut feel an almost mystical quality. Others attributed it to their emotions; still others attributed it directly to their brains, claiming that their gut feel was the result of a rigorous, expertise-driven set of schemas, mental models, and prototypes—conceptual ways of organizing that we'll get into later in the book. Some talked about how they trusted their gut feel. Others shared how their gut feel was dangerous and led them down the wrong track and totally derailed them. Most could not explain or articulate their gut feel. But once they understood how their personal experience and external data interacted in transcendent ways, and learned to listen to what whispers and not what screams, they could recognize, diagnose, trust, and rely upon their gut feel.

Part I of this book focuses on the *what* (and, as we'll soon see, the *who*) of intuition and gut feel. We'll discuss what intuition and gut feel are, how they interrelate, and why gut feel is so powerful—under the right conditions. We'll learn how gut feel manifests as a Eureka moment, a Spidey Sense, or a Jolt. And we'll discover how we not only can recognize when we've arrived at a gut feel that we can trust and act upon—all by understanding and reflecting on the process leading up to it—and also allow it to be the final arbiter. Part I covers those first two passes in the basketball drill—getting a sense for the intuitive process and beginning to diagnose what gut feel is. It also begins to tackle those third and fourth passes, recognizing how our personal experiences and external data interact to provide us with tremendous powers and capacities.

Part I will lay the groundwork in establishing the characteristics that define gut feel. We start here because it's what is most immediately recognizable and what we all have in common. We all know what it's like to experience a gut feel, so it's the most accessible point of entry. It's like introducing the primary colors—red, yellow, and blue—so that we can begin to recognize our individual inclination toward magenta, rose, coral, or cerise. This initial step ensures that we have a shared vocabulary and a foundational understanding of the core concepts.

Part II of the book—the fifth and sixth passes—take us to the *how* of gut feel, the realm of action and beyond. We're now equipped to go on a deeper exploration and analysis of our own intuiting process. We revisit and reflect upon our own experiences of gut feel, past the commonalities we hold, as we recognize the specific physical, emotional, and cognitive signals that are unique to each of us. This enables us to increase the volume and reliability of these signals as well as sharpen our sensitivity to them as we chart our own path to mastering our intuition and acting on our gut feel. We'll learn the difference between information and wisdom and how we need to be able to put together the right information at the right time, think critically about it, and make important choices wisely. Each chapter includes exercises that will enable you to put these ideas into practice. In part II, it will become apparent *how*—not just *why*—your personal experiences and external data are both important and how the interactions of the two will lead you to startling and invaluable breakthroughs in all facets of work and life—breakthroughs that are not only awe-inspiring but also completely trustworthy and transformative.

Now, dear reader, it's critical to note that on this journey of mastering our intuition, it may feel messy at times. There's no straightforward way to do this. Books, including this one, are read in a linear fashion, but our intuitive decision-making is anything but. Our brains function through a highly complex and dynamic network of neurons, which communicate via synapses, where neurotransmitters are released, creating electrical impulses that can fire in multiple directions simultaneously. It's precisely because of this nonlinear, parallel processing that our brains can handle vast amounts of information, integrate sensory inputs, make decisions, and generate thoughts and actions in a remarkably efficient and flexible manner.

Likewise, our emotions don't follow a linear path. They are influenced by various stimuli and arise from a complex interplay of neural circuits and biochemical processes involving multiple regions of the brain, such as the amygdala, prefrontal cortex, and hippocampus. They can be multifaceted, overlapping, and rapidly changing, reflecting the nuanced and interconnected nature of our emotional experiences.

And our bodies do not function in a linear manner either. Multiple interdependent physiological processes occur simultaneously, with the nervous, endocrine, and circulatory systems communicating constantly to maintain homeostasis. This intricate coordination ensures that responses to stimuli, such as stress or exercise, are rapid and multifaceted, demonstrating the dynamic nature of our bodily functions.

Our intuiting process constantly draws on physical, emotional, and cognitive inputs. Each piece may seem distinct, but they are intricately intertwined, creating a constant push-and-pull, a back-

and-forth that shapes our choices. There isn't necessarily a beginning, middle, and end. It's a holistic integration of what we know, what we feel, and what our bodies sense, leading to decisions that are deeply informed by the full spectrum of our human experience, compelling us to action. This is the challenge of quantifying the unquantifiable.

But we're going to do so, because the payoff will be extraordinary. Are you ready?

PART I

Intuition
and
Gut Feel

1

Intuition Is a Process, Gut Feel an Outcome

Gut feel is a flash of clarity resulting from an intuiting process that draws on the interaction of personal experience and external data.

In the late 1990s, the first-ever web page* was created by Tim Berners-Lee, sparking the beginning of the Internet Age. As the World Wide Web started to evolve and internet users began to grapple with the significance of immediately available, universally broad access to information, Ethan Zuckerman, who was an employee at tripod.com† and in charge of the design and implementation of the website, was contending with his own quandary. Web page–hosting sites, including tripod.com, couldn't quite figure out their revenue model. While advertisers seemed willing to pay, they were unhappy about how their ads appeared side by side with website content that would be associated with their brands.

Sometimes the content was irrelevant and disconnected, like in the case of advertisements from employment agencies about job

---

* The first *genuine* web page. The internet is said to have been officially invented a few years prior, but the late 1990s were when Tim Berners-Lee created what is now referred to as HTML code and used it to build a web page, marking the origin of the World Wide Web.
† One of the first successful dot-com companies.

opportunities in health care being placed next to articles about real estate investments. Other times, however, ads would be placed next to content that was disparaging, inappropriate, or downright offensive, which resulted in numerous complaints from advertisers.

Zuckerman had been pondering this issue for months, looking through ideas he had scribbled on Post-it notes, when he had a realization: Ads needed to be seen and couldn't be hidden because clicking between pages was too clunky. But they had to be less prominent and invasive. Why couldn't they be like his Post-it notes? As he stared at his computer, he pictured a Post-it note on his screen, covering just a tiny portion of it—big enough to notice but small enough to be able to focus on everything else on his screen. A few moments later, he scribbled down:

```
window.open('http://tripod.com/navbar.html'"
width=200, height=400,
toolbar=no, scrollbars=no,
resizable=no, target=_top");
```

It was a pop-up ad. He had a sudden sense of certainty—a gut feel—that this was *the* solution.

When you visited a Tripod page, the instructions embedded in the code he had written would spawn a small pop-up ad in its own window. It was technically separate—and hence not associated—with the particular page that it overlaid.

He couldn't contain his excitement. This weird, hacky solution was going to change the entire web experience. "It was a way to associate an ad with a user's page without putting it directly on the page, which advertisers worried would imply an association between their brand and the page's content," Zuckerman explained.

Today, pop-up ads hold an undeniable place in the history of online advertising. Not only did they solve the attention and association issues that Zuckerman was originally trying to figure out but they addressed the dwindling banner ad click-through rates that were also plaguing the industry. Pop-up ads saved online advertising and allowed companies to capture the attention of increasingly ad-blind users, and they translated to real ROI, where advertisers could start to determine if their ads were actually driving tangible results for their businesses. As a result, today marketers can more efficiently manage their campaigns across multiple websites. They're able to report on how users are interacting with their ads, make changes to a live campaign, reach their audience in hyper-targeted ways, and, in turn, pay according to search and pay-per-click through new pricing models based on cost per impression (CPM).

For those of us on the receiving end of these pop-up ads, they are a nuisance. Indeed, pop-ups have been called everything from "the most hated advertising technique" to "the internet's original sin." Google *pop-ups*, and you'll see that the top results all try to address questions like "How do I stop pop-ups?" "How do I block pop-ups?" and "How do I disable pop-ups?" Zuckerman has even apologized for creating the underlying code that unleashed them upon unsuspecting web surfers, despite his good intentions.

What Is Gut Feel?

It might seem like pop-ups came to Ethan Zuckerman as an immediate impulse. This impulse, however, was actually the result of an extensive process that began with a cocktail of familiarity and newness, and external data and personal experience, that gave rise to a pause, and then a sensation, and then a moment of clarity and certainty when he finally scribbled down that tiny snippet of code that would go on to change everyone's experience of web browsing forever.

How did Zuckerman know that he was in the midst of a breakthrough? And how can we create similar moments of breakthrough in our lives?

To answer these questions, we must first answer—and really answer—the question of "*What is gut feel?*" Let me ask you: What has been your definition up until now? Have you thought of gut feel as something good? Bad? Smart? Foolish? Rational? Emotional? Does it allow you to merely *blink* and know that an ancient statue in the Getty Museum is a fake, as Malcolm Gladwell would describe? Or is it something you see as fickle and undependable because our brains are lazy, relying on heuristics and error-laden shortcuts, as Daniel Kahneman claimed in *Thinking, Fast and Slow*? Do you think it depends? If so, what does it depend on?

I believe that the reason there is so much disagreement and debate on the nature of gut feel is because we've been trying to answer two questions at once. We've confused gut feel with intuition and used these terms interchangeably. I argue that, although they are related, they are distinct from each other.

Gut feel is a flash of clarity. It's a sudden moment of insight from deep within that often cannot be completely explained, yet inspires a strong sense of conviction, faith, and assurance.

Intuition is a mode of processing nonsequential information. Intuition is a process that can be short or long, during which information is accessed, and external data (as inputs) interact with your personal knowledge and experience, to enable you to form a judgment or make a decision. Intuition is the process; the outcome is the flash of clarity that we recognize as our gut feel. One is the process; the other is the outcome. Related yet distinct.

During this process—consider the word *intuition* synonymous with the term *intuiting process*—we are accessing information that we've stored in our long-term memory, information that we've acquired through associated learning, information induced by exposure to available options, and even information through unconscious cognition.

Although we experience gut feel—which is synonymous in my mind with *gut feel outcome* or *gut feel breakthrough*—as a sudden flash, it requires time to mature and it requires the intuitive process that leads up to the discrete moment of clarity and recognition. Those months that Zuckerman spent pondering the problem of his online advertisement, gathering information and thinking through solutions, were a necessary condition for arriving at his Eureka moment. His understanding happened gradually over the course of those months, even though the answer came suddenly, in a moment. We often don't recognize it that way because we tend to experience it instantly, as opposed to as a culmination of a process.

Judith Orloff, in her book *The Power of Intuition*, says: "Gut feelings are those rapid, physical responses that we sometimes get, which guide our immediate decisions. Intuition, however, is subtler and often involves a process of unconscious reasoning that informs our insights and judgments." She differentiates between the process and the outcome but doesn't go as far as to explicitly state that gut feel *is* the outcome. Similarly, Brené Brown, of *Daring Greatly* fame, concurs: "While gut feelings can be impulsive and reactionary, intuition is a quieter, more contemplative process that often requires time to reveal its insights." Gerd Gigerenzer, author of *Gut Feelings:*

The Intelligence of the Unconscious, comes the closest by declaring that intuition involves a deeper level of cognition and understanding, integrating past experiences and knowledge, with gut feel the response (to this).

Some think that gut feel is part of emotional intelligence and vice versa. Daniel Goleman, one of the foundational scholars of emotional intelligence, has discussed how gut feelings provide the basis of extracting life experiences to apply to any emotional sense of purpose, meaning, or ethics and vice versa. In this way, gut feel is related to emotional intelligence. Peter Salovey and John Mayer, also considered pioneers in the field of emotional intelligence, state that people with lower emotional intelligence tend to misread their own bodily signals and somatic cues. They sometimes misinterpret what their gut feel is trying to tell them. But gut feel goes beyond emotional intelligence. When honed, emotional intelligence can help us understand our experiences, background, lived truths, memories, emotions, and trauma in a way that informs our gut feel.

Many misunderstand gut feel as a mystical, instant panacea that will *just tell us* the answer. Or, at the other extreme, dismiss it and cite examples where data *and data alone* reigns supreme—like in the instance of "Moneyball," the sabermetric approach that used analytical, evidence-based information to recruit and build a baseball team, pioneered by Billy Beane and Peter Brand of the Oakland A's.*

Stories like Moneyball seem to leave us with the conclusion: Don't rely on your gut. Rely on the data. Data doesn't lie. The story is an argument for rigorous statistical analysis and data eclipsing all else.

Yet what was so interesting to me was that Billy Beane's team

---

* And glorified by Brad Pitt and Jonah Hill of Hollywood fame.

didn't start doing well until he got to know his players and engaged with them, drawing on his own experiences as a player. The data was critical, and the analytics did reshape the game—but only when he realized that the experience of a manager still had a place in the game.

Indeed, researcher David De Cremer and chess grand master and World Chess Champion Garry Kasparov looked into this amalgam of data and experience and found that even with all the fanfare about how AI, machine learning, and data-centric modeling will change the nature of decision-making, it's only when AI and human intelligence augment each other that we truly see breakthroughs. In 1997 IBM's Deep Blue computer defeated Kasparov, leading to decades of discussion about the power of data and artificial intelligence vis-à-vis human intelligence. But out of Kasparov's defeat came his investigation into the type of chess player who would dominate. His conclusion: the centaur chess player. Neither man alone nor machine alone. Mike Cassidy, who has studied this interplay between humans and machines, describes a centaur chess player as "one who plays the game by marrying human intuition, creativity and empathy with a computer's brute-force ability to remember and calculate a staggering number of chess moves, countermoves and outcomes." It's by combining data with personal experience, over the course of a *process* in which players and computers are interacting, that leads to the best outcome. As Kasparov describes, "Weak human + machine + better process is superior to a strong computer alone and, more remarkably, superior to a strong human + machine + inferior process."

The outcome is reliant on the strength of the process. The reliability of your gut feel is dependent on the quality of your intuiting process.

It was the analytics, combined with "feeling" the game, that led to success for Billy Beane as well. Both data and scout player evaluations helped them quantify the intangibles and build a team. It's individuals who ultimately need to interpret the data, slice and dice it in operative ways, integrate it into what you already know, make decisions, and act on them—whether you're in baseball, chess, or business.

This is why I often say that the more important question isn't necessarily "*What is gut feel?*" but "*Who is gut feel?*" And by answering *this* question, we'll be able to grasp a richer, fuller definition that will allow us to develop our ability to reach intentional breakthroughs: *Gut feel is a flash of clarity resulting from an intuiting process that draws on the interaction of personal experience and external data.*

Who Is Gut Feel?

If gut feel is the outcome and intuition is the process, then there must be an individual in whom this is taking place. Gut feel is you. As a professor, I often say to my students: "The most beautiful story you ever tell should be the story of who you are and the collection of all you love." Gut feel is informed by the entirety of your lived experience: your knowledge, observations, background, memories, truths, relationships, feelings, emotional intelligence, disappointments, losses, and trauma. Gut feel is you because it stems from your individual interpretation of the external data that you are receiving and acquiring, and it is the culmination of everything that takes place during your intuiting process. The gut feel breakthroughs you have will be distinct and personal, specific just to you. They cannot be explained;* they cannot be transferred.

---

* Though the gut feel breakthrough cannot, the intuiting process leading up to it can be somewhat explained.

For this reason, once you fully comprehend, recognize, and harness it, you can use it to make the right decisions and act on them, with a greater chance of success. You can learn how to rely on past experiences, thoughts, emotions, tendencies—everything that makes us unique and makes us who we are—to master the intuiting process that leads to gut feel breakthroughs that you can undeniably trust. Understanding that gut feel is you allows you to discover that there is also a unique, personal way you experience it. Just like there are different body types, so too are there individual idiosyncrasies in how our gut feel breakthroughs manifest.

Over the course of this book, we will hone and master our intuiting process, and sharpen the recognition and activation of our gut feel so that it becomes a reliable superpower that drives our success. For that to happen, we need to listen closely to ensure it isn't drowned out by the noise around us—recognizing that another important characteristic of gut feel is that it can be quiet and unassuming and quite easy to snub. You may already be feeling the urge to move to the intuiting process and consider your own intuitive patterns. But hold that impulse because we're not done laying the groundwork. We'll continue discussing the outcome of intuition—gut feel—so we can better grasp and master both the experience of arriving at a conclusion, however quiet, as well as the nonlinear process leading up to it, more effectively.

2

Gut Feel Is Not Easily Heard

Listen to what whispers
and not what screams.

Surigao City in the Philippines is known as the City of Island Adventures because of its seventeen beautiful islands, each with long stretches of pristine white-sand beaches, underwater marvels, mystical caves, and massive mangrove forests. One of my students grew up there. I said to him, "You must have amazing childhood memories of beaches and island adventures." He shook his head and then shared that his most powerful memories were not of the stunning natural beauty but of boats and killer typhoons. "As a child," he shared, "I learned the most important life and business lesson: 'Ships don't sink because of the water around them; ships sink because of the water that gets in them.' It always reminds me that you can't let what's happening around you get inside of you and weigh you down."

The Inner Voice

Our gut feel whispers to us, and we don't often listen. We're too distracted by everything that is screaming at us during the intuiting process—the people in our lives (some welcome, some not), voices in both traditional and social media, the chores and responsibilities of daily living, and all that we must contend with on a regular basis.

When we try to make decisions, what is it that we often do? We ask people whom we trust for their opinions. We seek out sources of knowledge and insight. We look around to see what others have done, and we compare ourselves to them. This can all be a part of the intuiting process, but there is often contradictory information from different sources, with each trying to talk over the other. This can get very noisy, with the din growing increasingly louder. Your head is whipping from person to person, from idea to idea.

At some point, there will be a quiet voice, whispering to you from within. This is our inner voice—our gut feel—that has accumulated wisdom, opinions, information, and perceptions throughout the intuiting process, and we would do well to listen.

There are two ways to improve our chances of "hearing" our inner voice. The first is by amplifying it—adjusting, maneuvering, and manipulating the whisper so that it is audible and clear to us. The second is by tuning in to it—noticing the natural properties of our whisper so that we are listening more intentionally and proactively. In fields such as electrical engineering, telecommunications, and neuroscience, these two methods are akin to signal amplification on the one hand, which involves increasing the power of a signal without significantly distorting its content, and noise reduction on the other, which allows you to hear the signal by minimizing unwanted ambient or background sounds.

We'll start with the first, which is more straightforward, though it can be much more jarring, as experienced by Shai, a former student of mine. Prior to being one of my brightest MBA students,* Shai was a leader in one of the top military special forces units in the world. Competition to serve in this unit is fierce, and cadets who are nominated for it go through a long training process. First, they undergo physical and mental tests. Those who pass are subjected to another week of tests on basic infantry, fieldcraft and field navigation in different terrains, counterinsurgency, air-to-ground cooperation, airborne operations, intelligence gathering, sharpshooter acumen, medical skills, psychological character, mental stability, and more. Afterward, they are assigned to units where they train as infantry soldiers.

Shai's job as a team leader was to determine who among his team of twenty-four cadets, or infantry soldiers, would make the cut. "There wasn't any particular number that I had to choose. But you chose carefully . . . because these were guys that would be in combat with you. Your life would be on the line while they were next to you. . . . One guy, he had the heart. He had sacrificed a lot. And I really struggled on what to do about him."

Shai told me that one of his superiors said to him, "Just flip a coin." His first reaction to these words (which he said out loud) was a shocked "*What?* Make a decision like this by flipping a coin?"

His commanding officer replied, "No, not to make the decision itself, but to get the sensation. What kind of sensation are you getting? . . . When heads tells you to cut the guy, how does that make you feel?"

I told Shai that it reminded me of an episode of the TV show *Friends* when Rachel finds out she's pregnant. He remembered this

---

* Whoever said that teachers are not designed to be students' best friends was just wrong. I much prefer the sentiment from this quote: "Today, my friend, the student has become the teacher."

episode, too, and we chuckled at its resemblance to what he had just shared.[*]

In the episode, Rachel thinks she is pregnant and is freaking out. She confides in her friend Phoebe, who tells her to calm down because it's possible that the pregnancy test she took earlier was a false positive and she should take another one to be sure. Rachel does just that, and as they're in the bathroom waiting for the outcome of the second test, Rachel asks Phoebe to tell her the results because she's too nervous to look. Phoebe takes a look, and announces, "Um, it's negative." Rachel pauses at this news, and then mutters, "Oh. Oh. Well, there you go. Phew!" (pause) "That is . . . That's great . . . That is really great, great news." (pause) "You know . . . 'cause the whole not being ready and . . . kinda . . . the financial aspects, all that. Phew. Phew. Wow, this is so just the way it was supposed to be."

At this point, Rachel starts to cry. Phoebe gives her a tissue, and Rachel continues, "Thanks." (crying) "God, this is so stupid!" (pause) "How could I be upset over something I never had?" (pause) "It's . . . it's negative?"

Not skipping a beat, Phoebe says, "No, it's positive," to which Rachel responds, "What?!" Phoebe repeats, "It's . . . it's not negative. It's positive."

As Rachel asks Phoebe, "Are . . . are you sure?" Phoebe quickly quips, "Well, yeah, I lied before!" Phoebe sees that her friend is stunned but clearly relieved and happy and says, "Now you know how you really feel about it." Rachel retorts, "Well that was a risky little game!" Then she excitedly starts hugging Phoebe and shout-

---

[*] We also laughed about how we had to watch shows like *Friends* "live" when it was on every Thursday night. None of this Netflix binge-watching, which actually prevents us from absorbing and processing information that helps us harness our gut feel. More on that later.

ing, "I'm gonna have a baby! I'm gonna have a baby! I'm gonna have a baby!"

Getting to the "In the Moment" Moment

As soon as Shai and Rachel learned (or forced) the outcome, they felt a sensation.

When "heads" told Shai that he'd cut the cadet, he felt relief, and that sensation was a signal to him. His feeling was based on an integration of many moments and experiences that had come before, all of the inputs: Being in combat is indescribable. Putting someone in combat is a huge responsibility. This was a cadet that he had pulled for and trusted, someone who had sacrificed a lot. But even though this individual had tried his hardest, his ability to make the cut and protect others gave Shai pause because it would put the other infantry soldiers at risk.* All these inputs were distilled into a single sensation for him that amplified and clarified the whisper. He saw that all the moments leading up to the outcome of the coin flip matched what he actually felt and knew deep down.†

Similarly, when Phoebe told Rachel that she was actually pregnant (after previously informing her that she wasn't),‡ Rachel's relief,

---

* Many of the top military programs in the world train their soldiers to learn how to sit in and be okay with uncertainty, as well as to be incredibly fast thinkers. Beyond Shai, I've gotten to know a number of people who have served in the military, and they make decisions quickly (and get impatient quickly) because they've learned that when they see the path forward, there is no need to waffle.

† We don't know the counterfactual. But that was his gut feel, and it was powerful.

‡ It was a smart but risky little stunt on the part of Phoebe. There was a lot of debate among the *Friends* fan base about whether Phoebe was being too clever and how it could have blown up in her face had the outcome been different. But Phoebe had a sense of how Rachel felt and was very intuitive in providing Rachel with the type of clarity that she needed.

disappointment, tears, joy, past relationships, experiences as a daughter all came flooding into a moment of confrontation with her true feelings: her excitement at the prospect of becoming a mother. It amplified and clarified her inner voice.

Like Shai and Rachel, we can pump up the volume of the whisper by forcing a gut feel—the sensation that comes at the end of the intuiting process during which all the personal experience and data that we've accumulated along the way coalesces. Unlike them, who had to be brought to their moment of reckoning by others (Shai's commanding officer and Phoebe) because they had been in an intuiting process for a while—perhaps too long—we can do it more intentionally. We can learn how to amplify it on our own by doing the equivalent of a coin flip. But we need to know the right moment to force a gut feel—once we've finished effectively filtering information, making sense of our experiences, and interpreting our observations. It's like knowing when all the grains, fruits, and sugars that we have fermented, concentrated, filtered, and purified have produced the finest distilled spirit.

Never Drink the Route 66

Speaking of the perfect liquor, let me tell you what I think is the exact opposite. When I was in grad school, there was a local bar that we'd frequent, and at the end of the night, during last call, they'd offer a drink called the Route 66 on the house. All night, bartenders would be mixing cocktails, topping them off with a squeeze of lime or an extra cherry, pouring wine, popping off beer-bottle caps—all on top of bar spill mats that were long, thin reservoirs for any liquids spilled from overpours, shaking, or stirring.

Route 66 was created by carefully picking up that bar mat, angling it into a frozen glass, and pouring everything from the mat into the glass. It was disgusting—and yet we drank it.

Believe it or not, this is how we make a lot of our decisions. We base them on everything that is screaming at us—the metaphorical equivalent of those soaking spill mats—and go from there.

After I graduated, I never had another Route 66, nor would I ever in the future. I don't tell my MBA students about the drink (lest they get any ideas), but on the first day of class, I do give them some advice akin to how not to ever drink a Route 66.

I tell them to think of their MBA experience as if they're filling a paper cup. At the end of their two-year program, they get to take that paper cup and everything in it with them. They can fill their cup with anything they want, but all they get is one paper cup because that's the equivalent of what they cognitively, emotionally, practically, and humanly have the capacity to retain.

As they start to fill their cups, most notice that they've been provided with tons of opportunities and experiences—classes, classmates, professors, clubs, activities, sporting events, networking events, guest speakers, internships, travel opportunities, exposure to all sorts of people and topics—each a gushing water faucet. As they try to place their cups under faucet after faucet, there's water going in, but just as much pouring out. Yet they continue to run from faucet to faucet, trying to experience it all. At the end of their two years, they'll all have full cups, but they won't necessarily know exactly what's in it.

Instead, I tell them to figure out what they're trying to get out of the experience, what their goal is, what problem they're trying to solve. Once they do that, they turn each of those faucets, so they're dripping instead of gushing. And they can take their paper cups and put them under faucets of their choosing—taking ten drips of this, maybe sixty drips of that because it's really important to them, another five drips of something else, and maybe one or two drips from everything else to get some diversity of thought and experience. They leave knowing exactly what is in their paper cup. This is when they are ready to prime those whispers for the particular problem or question they're trying to solve.

In early 2020, I had a gut feel (or so I thought) about an investment opportunity. Had I acted on that gut feel, I would have lost a substantial amount of money. Instead, I realized that my paper cup was filled with irrelevant, useless, or duplicated information. I needed to be more intentional. I learned about the greed and fear index, and discovered that I was basing my decision on greed and the bandwagon effect, rather than on an understanding of the underlying asset. I talked to some experts and studied the industries in question. Two years later, I made my investment, and turned a profit.

You need to understand what is in your cup. Do you have personal experience that directly pertains to the decision at hand or is analogous or tangential to the problem? Do you have hard data and information related to the issue? Are they from reliable sources? Is it current or outdated? Is the information you have clear and comprehensible? Or is it ambiguous and confusing?

There are actually no right or wrong answers to these questions. The key is that you *know* the answers, whatever they might be. That's when the interaction of the external data vis-à-vis all your personal knowledge and experience produces a gut feel. That's when you choose to flip the coin to see how you feel about what it tells you to do. That's how you begin to master your intuition so the signal is more audible.*

Lest we forget, there is a second way to hear your inner voice, and that is by being more attuned to its properties and what it's trying to tell us. We can learn how those natural coin flip moments feel when they happen in the wild. They feel like the opposite of inertia, becoming catalysts that spur us to decision and action. We can become skilled at recognizing how our gut feel manifests. As we'll discover, our gut feel takes three forms—Eureka, Spidey Sense, and Jolt—each with its own sensations that are unique to us.

---

* Even in those instances when the answers to each of those questions is a resounding no, your gut feel is still telling you something. It's telling you that you need to keep gathering more relevant data. We'll discuss this at greater length in chapter 3.

3

Gut Feel Is Sensed in Three Ways

Water presents as liquid, solid, or gas. Our gut feel manifests in three forms too.

Water, the most abundant natural resource on earth, exists in three distinct forms: liquid, solid, and gas.* Gut feel, the most abundant natural resource for the decisions we make and the actions we take in life, also manifests in three distinct forms: aha moments (Eureka), uh-oh moments (Spidey Sense), and whoa moments (Jolts). Each is accompanied by a specific sensation that provides a signal of connection (Eureka), dissonance (Spidey Sense), or displacement (Jolt). Each has its own triggers and patterns of recognition. That is, we can distinguish between each of them and what they are trying to tell us, if we know what to look for.

Here is how Jack Dorsey, the founder of Twitter (now X), described his Eureka moment:

---

* Yes, I know there is also plasma. Let's be basic for now.

I was flipping through the dictionary, when my eyes came across a word that just leapt out at me. *Twitter*: "a short burst of inconsequential information," read the first definition. "A series of short chirps from birds," read the next. Eureka! Perfect descriptors for the product I was building, and I just had this feeling that this word would not only become the name of my new company but would change my life.

Eureka moments are about confirmation, where something that we newly experience causes us to sit up and take notice because of how well it just *fits* and connects.

Lauren Vriens, AI strategist and founder of Habit and Co., was looking to fill a critical position when her Spidey Sense was triggered during the hiring process:

> Every single person on my team—each of whom I trusted completely—had interviewed Tina and raved about how smart she was, how fitting she was for the role. I met her and couldn't deny that she had all the right experience for what we were looking for. And so I hired her—even though the entire time I was doing so, I felt an ominous feeling that I couldn't shake. It was only months later, as I was sifting through the disastrous sequence of actions that Tina had taken—actions that destroyed our company— that I realized the importance of that mismatch in energy and how I should have listened to my Spidey Sense.

Having a Spidey Sense is different from a Eureka moment, even though both are catalysts, moments when you hear your inner voice. With a Spidey Sense, that new piece of information *doesn't* fit with what we know and understand. It feels like something is off, so it makes us uncomfortable or agitated in some way.

Former Head Chef of Noma and founder and CEO of Brigaid Dan Giusti's Jolt led him to a new purpose:

> I came across an article—I don't even remember reading it in full—but the words *institutional food* popped out to me. I felt a Jolt, a shift in my core. Here I was, in Copenhagen, Denmark, the head chef, chef de cuisine, at three-starred Michelin restaurant Noma, named best restaurant in the world. I was at the apex of a career in food and gastronomy, but I quit that life so that I could instead cook for and bring my culinary expertise to school cafeterias, prison inmates, and sick people in hospitals.

We experience a Jolt when something that we always knew or held to be true is dislodged and called into question. Distinct from a Eureka moment, which confirms what you already knew, Jolts *change* what you thought you knew. That new piece of information introduces a fresh way of seeing things, a new belief system, a paradigm shift.

Check Your Priors

To truly understand the differences among Eureka, Spidey Sense, and Jolt, we need to go deeper. We need to understand what is triggering each sensation by recognizing what type of dance your personal experience and the external data are engaged in during the intuiting process leading up to your gut feel.

Your experience is in the form of *priors*: They are things you know, things you know you know, and things you don't know you know. The data comes in the form of *prompts*: They are things you don't know.

When there is a match between your priors and the prompts, Eureka. When there is a prompt that is a mismatch with your priors, Spidey Sense. And when your priors are being displaced entirely, there's a Jolt. The sensations we receive come from how our priors and our prompts collide.

This is why it's so important to prioritize your priors, for they shape your prompts. And in the prompts lies the power to shape your path. Let me step back for a second to explain.

In statistics, what are often referred to as priors is short for something called the *prior probability distribution*. Priors come from a branch of statistics called Bayesian statistics,* which focuses on beliefs,† or more specifically, how you express your degree of belief in an event occurring. This might come from prior knowledge that you have (having experienced it in the past or having tested it in the past) or your beliefs (in what you've heard, observed, or internalized). It might come from what you're currently thinking about or ruminating over, as introspection is also about examining your priors. You might have a pretty strong belief that you'll get sick if you eat raw cookie dough, for instance, because you've gotten food poisoning in the past after eating a spoonful of raw cookie dough, because you've actually tested the difference in how you feel after eating a baked cookie versus a raw cookie, or because your mother told you so many times during childhood that you'd get sick if you ate raw cookie dough.

---

* My favorite branch, if you could say such a thing out loud and still maintain your dignity outside of academia.
† The *B* stands for *Bayesian* and *beliefs*.

This is the *prior* information that comes into play at the exact moment that someone is offering you a lick of the spoon. Those are your priors: things you know, or things you think you know, even if they're just misguided assumptions.

Then you have prompts, which are experienced in the moment. It's when you're being asked if you want to lick the spoon that is covered in cookie dough. In this case, the prompt is presented to you. Prompts can also be sought out. For example, you might be looking for something tasty to eat and then happen upon someone baking cookies in the kitchen.

Something special can happen in the moment when your priors meet a prompt—that is, if you don't completely ignore that moment of gut feel that might tell you: *Don't eat the cookie dough. You'll get sick.* This is *the* moment when your intuiting process naturally produces (concludes with) a gut feel breakthrough.

Priors + Prompts = Gut Feel

It's the moment facilitated by Shai's coin flip, in instances when your gut feel is induced. Don't eat the cookie dough? That's your Spidey Sense. Your response to the prompt is *Uh-oh!* You're experiencing dissonance. Something doesn't fit between what you think you know (*don't eat the dough!*) and what you're being presented with (*eat the cookie dough!*). Your priors are telling you that eating cookie dough leads to sickness, so you refuse the prompt.

Someone else might not have a Spidey Sense at all and instead have a Jolt. They might feel something dislodge from their memory and in that moment, think, *Why* shouldn't *I eat the cookie dough? Whoa, everything my mother told me about cookie dough leading to salmonella was an old wives' tale. It's not going to do any real damage.*

What makes this a Jolt is that the prompt has brought about a change in their priors or what that person always thought they knew and believed.

And then, of course, there might be someone who has a Eureka moment. A light bulb might go off, an *aha*, and they might decide, then and there, that they need to invent a safe cookie dough, for example, with no raw egg ingredients and hence no risk of food sickness. Their priors and this prompt aligned and helped them see an opportunity that just clicked.

The Four Quadrants

		PRIORS	
		✅	❗
PROMPT	✅	**Eureka** A feeling of **Connection** *The prompt aligns with my priors.*	**Jolt** A feeling of **Displacement** *The prompt dislodges my priors.*
	❗	**Spidey Sense** A feeling of **Dissonance** *The prompt doesn't align with my priors.*	*The prompt doesn't align with my priors, but I'm still intuiting. I need more data. I need to continue to experience more.*

Decisions about cookie dough are obviously not the most profound ones we're going to make. The point is, for any decision we're going to be faced with, there are priors, things we know from our lived experience, and prompts, things we are newly confronted with. It could be new because we're seeing it for the first time, it could be some piece of information that we've gathered or sought out, it could be a new fact or figure that we've just read, or it could be any type of feedback, signal, or cue that someone is giving us. These prompts push us to check our priors. They help us engage in the sensemaking that is required to arrive at a gut feel.

Eureka moments result when the brain connects the prompt to our priors—information that previously seemed unrelated—leading to a sudden insight or realization. It's as if a mental puzzle piece falls into place, providing a new idea or solution. This is the brain engaging in pattern recognition and creative problem-solving. (Later in the book, we'll discuss how we can proactively help our brain make these connections.)

When experiencing a Eureka moment, the telltale sign is a sudden sense of clarity or understanding, accompanied by a feeling of excitement or satisfaction.

This is what happened to Ethan Zuckerman. Remember Zuckerman, the one who invented pop-up ads? He had a Eureka moment. He was prompted when he glanced over and saw his Post-it notes. This prompt wasn't intentionally sought out but was instead the slightest of accidents (provocations) that led to a moment of pause, when he made the connection between what he was seeing (the Post-it notes) and his priors (his understanding that ads needed to be seen but not associated with the website's content). During his Eureka moment, he was transported to a higher plane of understanding and insight.

Spidey Sense moments occur when the prompt doesn't align with our priors. The brain recognizes the potential risks and negative outcomes of a prompt based on our past experiences, cues, or subconscious assessments. When encountering a situation that triggers our Spidey Senses, we experience discomfort, unease, or a sense of caution. This emotional response compels us to pause, take note, and act accordingly—sometimes in very profound and life-altering ways.

Jolts are those moments when the prompt dislodges our priors, and we realize something we always thought we knew is wrong. Jolts arise from the brain's capacity to adapt and change its mental frameworks in response to new and disruptive information. It involves the brain's ability to challenge existing assumptions and beliefs when presented with contradictory evidence. When experiencing a Jolt, we feel a flood or rush, like we're spatially turned around, completely knocked off our feet, or in a different dimension. Whereas Eureka moments are a positive feedback loop and Spidey Senses warn us something isn't right, Jolts result in a paradigm shift. This can lead to questioning long-held beliefs, considering new possibilities, and embracing innovative, similarly life-changing approaches.

There is a fourth quadrant where there is a mismatch between the prompt and your priors, but you're still in the intuiting process. You need more data. That's okay. Your cup's not full yet, remember? Or maybe you're still in the intuiting process and you need to let yourself sit in that space longer. You need more information. Remember, this is a messy, nonlinear process where intuition and gut feel are in a constant state of push and pull, and being able to register that is powerful in its own right. Even though it's not a gut feel (yet), it's an important signal to recognize nonetheless. Too many people take action when they are in this quadrant, and that's a mistake.* But it's a mistake that you won't make, for reasons that we'll see in the next chapters as we continue to build our understanding of gut feel and the characteristics that define this "outcome" of intuition.

---

* "Be curious, not judgmental," said Ted Lasso.

4

Gut Feel Doesn't Lie

For complex and chaotic problems,
gut feel can always be trusted.

Rick Cohen is the president and CEO of C&S Wholesale Grocers, one of the largest grocery wholesalers in the United States. C&S purchases products in bulk from food manufacturers and sells them to various supermarkets and convenience stores where people buy their groceries. It was October, and the holiday season was only a few weeks away. They had just landed a huge new customer, from whom they were expecting large orders, but they were already feeling overstretched. Rick was worried about their ability to meet the needs of their new customer as well as those of their existing customers and maintain high customer satisfaction.

Rick had a lot of existing mental models, schemas, and prototypes (conceptual ways of organizing) based on his experience (priors), and he was confident in the following information:

- The company had been around for a long time (it was founded in 1918), and it's a major player in the grocery distribution industry.

- Distribution centers are critical to the business. C&S operates a network of distribution centers and facilities across the United States, and this extensive infrastructure allows the company to efficiently serve its diverse customer base in different regions.

- C&S has a wide product range, offering a comprehensive selection of grocery products, including both perishable and nonperishable items. Their inventory includes everything from fresh produce and dairy products to packaged foods and household goods.

- They have a wide customer base. Their customers are national and regional retail chains and independent grocery stores, and these businesses rely on the company to provide them with the products they need to stock their shelves.

- It's an operationally difficult business. There are tons of moving pieces and lots of people involved, from truckers who unload the products to loaders who shrink-wrap pallets and get them ready for grocery stores. Because it's not a glamorous job that doesn't have extremely high pay, there tends to be a lot of turnover.

From his priors, Rick had this process in the back of his head. He paused and noticed something—a sensation—that was related to this new customer and how it would represent a 35 percent increase in business. Rick experienced a few sensations, actually: a

Rick Cohen's Priors of the C&S Grocery Process

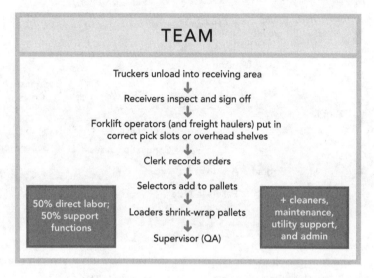

bit of anxiety about potentially not being able to successfully handle this new customer but also a feeling that perhaps he had been seeing the company's fundamental business model differently than it actually is.

He started to process questions like: *How do we (actually) compete in this business? How do we differentiate our business, on both cost and service? What are the margins in this business like? Why are competitors a threat?* And then he asked himself: *What do I do? Is this gut feel I'm having a negative or positive one?* It was definitely a negative one.

If I had to summarize my gut feel, what would be its tagline? Rick thought. His answer? *We are growing our way to decline.*

More business was coming in, but because the organization wasn't functioning optimally, the growth would actually undermine the company. Rick needed to decide how to stop this negative cycle, which he saw as a "circle of doom" or "death spiral."

Rick Cohen's Priors of C&S Operational Challenges

The root problem was employee turnover. The more growth they experienced, the more new workers they needed. The more workers they had, the more training they required, but the less they could keep up with. More employees and less training led to more congestion, errors, and accidents. This reduced performance required more oversight, which resulted in declining morale. That led to even higher turnover, which would launch the entire cycle anew.

This was Rick's intuiting process. As observers, we can see that Rick was diagnosing, analyzing, and developing all sorts of introspective conclusions along the way—even if he himself wasn't aware of it during that period of time.

What Rick does know and what he shared is that when the prompt (a giant new customer) encountered his priors (his knowledge about the company), he had a gut feel breakthrough: the realization that at the heart of his company were his employees, particularly the ones who had been there for decades and were seeing all this turnover, who were expected to train new workers instead of doing what they were unreservedly great at—taking care of customers. It was a gut feel that supported what he already knew: His *existing* employees were capable, excellent, and trustworthy. They had more institutional knowledge than he did. They should be shown their value. This realization didn't change how he fundamentally saw things. It underscored what he had known all along.

Rick took quick action. He put *self-managed teams* in place. Employees would work collaboratively in teams with little to no direct supervision.

He knew that there would be risks: The lack of supervision could impact the quality of work. There would be potential for abuse. It may make it hard for new employees to be accepted. But Rick also knew that he'd be able to create the right conditions for the self-managed teams to function well. He would ensure that the team selection process would be equitable, that team members would have complementary skills, that the objectives and expectations would be clear and common across teams, that the incentive structure and metrics would be fair and known to everyone, and that the teams would have (and trust that they'd have) the authority to manage their work.

It was a huge success. Self-managed teams allowed for astronomically greater productivity, and C&S moved more cases per hour than they ever had before. Compensation was tied directly to team performance, not individual performance, and teams competed against each other, creating scoreboards and their own performance metrics. Employee pay rose to unprecedented heights, and the company was able to sustain it because there were fewer supervisors on staff. Group monitoring was more effective than supervisory control, and workers delighted in being able to make decisions quickly and efficiently because they didn't need to wait for approval from higher levels of management. This agility was especially valuable in a fast-paced industry like grocery distribution. With greater autonomy and ownership over their own work, employees felt empowered and took pride in the job. This led to lower turnover and higher morale.

Team members were more willing to share their expertise and best practices, which led to continuous improvement in processes and operations, helping the company stay competitive. There was a built-in mechanism for regularly assessing their performance, making adjustments, and using creative solutions and innovation to enhance efficiency and effectiveness. The self-managed teams could also be more customer focused. Closer to the front lines of service, they could make decisions that prioritized customer satisfaction and respond promptly to customer feedback at their discretion. They were also more adaptable and were able to respond to change with greater agility—especially in moments of tragedy.

On the morning of 9/11, Rick Cohen received a call from a twenty-eight-year-old team member at the Brooklyn distribution center: "Mr. Cohen, turn on your TV because there's an emergency in New York." After seeing less than a minute of the news, Rick said, "Do whatever you need to do." Ninety minutes later, twenty-five C&S trucks were on their way down the West Side Highway full of water and power bars. They were the first trucks to arrive.

Similarly, after Hurricane Katrina made landfall along the Gulf Coast on August 29, 2005, taking more than 1,800 lives, destroying more than eight hundred thousand housing units, and leaving thousands homeless, a twenty-five-year-old employee called Rick from the Birmingham site and said, "Mr. Cohen, there's an emergency." Rick replied, "Do what you need to do." The twenty-five-year-old responded, "We know here in the South that when you have too much water, you need water." Right before twenty C&S

trucks full of water were ready to leave Birmingham, another team member said, "You know, we ought to throw on some baby food so they have that too." The trucks full of water and baby food arrived ten hours before the federal government aid trucks.

While these examples are a testament to the success of C&S's self-managed teams, this was only possible because Rick Cohen relied on his priors and his deep understanding of the organization to lead him to an awareness and recognition of the right action.* Success resulted because his gut feel guided him to a counterintuitive solution (self-managed teams) to a *chaotic problem* (high turnover)—the type of problem that *required* his gut feel.

C&S Wholesale Grocers is now the largest grocery wholesaler in the United States, boasting $33 billion in annual revenue and fifteen thousand employees. It is the eighth-largest privately held company in the country—meaning that it's entirely owned by one or more founders, managers, private investors, and/or families, and because it's not publicly traded on a stock exchange and doesn't receive investments or capital from the public, decisions are made entirely by the owner. C&S Wholesale Grocers has a sole owner: Rick Cohen. He has a personal net worth of $12.7 billion. A very private man, he's the billionaire many of us have never heard of, quietly amassing his fortune—and relying on his gut feel.

The Most Honest Friend You'll Ever Have

There are two reasons why gut feel never lies. First, as we already know, is because gut feel is you. Your gut feel is always right because

---

* He believed in the veracity of his priors. In the coming chapters, we'll discuss what happens when you think that your priors might be incorrect or when you are trying to figure out what is and isn't correct.

it comes from you—or, I should say, it's always right *when* it comes from you and it's authentically you. That's not to say that we don't sometimes lie to ourselves during the intuiting process. But as long as you don't second-guess your own lived experiences, your priors, and allow yourself to invalidate them during the process by deferring to others' opinions and views and prioritizing them over what you distinctly know, things won't go awry. Your intuition will lead you to the right gut feel (or, as we'll discuss soon, you'll be equipped to fix and pivot on any gut feel decision you do make to ensure it's the right one).

It's important to note that this isn't to say that our priors are always correct. Remember, when we experience a Jolt, it's explicitly because we're undergoing a transformation where we've realized during the intuiting process that our priors were incorrect—sometimes very much so. But that conclusion is reached only when we've authentically owned and enfolded ourselves into understanding our priors and what they represent—rather than someone else's opinions and priors that do not mesh with our own.* It still came from you and your gut feel.

Similarly, it's not the case that trusting yourself means ignoring our own cognitive biases. We know from decades of research that biases exist and that we, as humans, are prone to making errors like only paying attention to news stories that confirm our own opinions (confirmation bias), or blaming outside factors when things don't go our way (fundamental attribution bias), or chalking up other people's success to luck but taking personal credit for our

---

* Prompts can sometimes take the form of someone else's opinions and priors. This is another case where we must acknowledge the messy, nonlinear nature of the intuiting process and why mastering our intuition (so that we recognize these subtle distinctions) is so important.

own accomplishments (self-serving bias). When these types of biases rear their ugly heads, there are ways in which we can be primed to address them—in our own way, rather than through a method that is uniquely someone else's. The key is to know your own conventions, patterns, fixations, and obsessions. Own your own good, bad, and ugly. It's when you forsake who you are and defer to, even prioritize, the guidance of others' voices, expectations, or approaches over your own that it gets tricky.

Second, gut feel never lies when we're operating in the realm of the complex and chaotic. To properly understand this, we'll need to examine the four types of problems.

The Four Types of Problems

The Cynefin framework* describes how we make sense of the world: There are simple, complicated, complex, and chaotic domains,† and these four domains represent the perspective from which we view any situation. *Cynefin* is the Welsh word for *habitat*, which is fitting because the framework describes the "sense of place" from which we view any decision-making context. When we're able to

---

* The framework is based on seminal works such as Russell L. Ackoff's *Scientific Method: Optimizing Applied Research Decisions* (Wiley, 1962), C. West Churchman's *Design of Inquiring Systems* (New York: Basic Books, 1971), Horst W. J. Rittel and Melvin M. Webber's "Dilemmas in a General Theory of Planning" (*Policy Sciences* 4, 1973): 155–69, Douglas John White's *Decision Methodology* (Wiley, 1975), John Tukey's *Exploratory Data Analysis* (Addison-Wesley, 1977), Michael Pidd's *Tools for Thinking: Modelling in Management Science* (Wiley, 1996), and Tom Ritchey's presentation of general morphological analysis in "Fritz Zwicky, 'Morphologie' and Policy Analysis" (Swedish Morphological Society, 1998).
† Dave Snowden, who first proposed the present form of the framework in 1999, has changed the domain names over the years. In 2003, Snowden and his colleague Cynthia Kurtz called them known, knowable, complex, and chaotic domains. Later, in 2007, known and knowable were changed to simple and complicated. A fifth domain—disorder—is sometimes used to describe situations where it is unclear which of the other four is predominant.

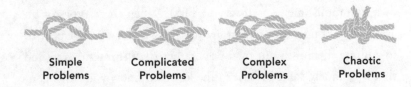

| Simple Problems | Complicated Problems | Complex Problems | Chaotic Problems |

diagnose whether a situation is simple, complicated, complex, or chaotic, then we can act in contextually appropriate ways and use the right tools* to solve the problem. As Robert H. Schuller once said, *"Problems are not stop signs; they are guidelines."*

Simple and complicated problems are "ordered," meaning cause and effect are known or can be discovered (knowable).

Simple problems are familiar and have a single solution: There are rules or best practices in place, the situation is well-defined and stable, and there is a clear, known cause-and-effect relationship (if you do x, you can expect y). For example, a health care provider who is treating a patient who has tested positive for strep throat would prescribe antibiotics, typically penicillin or amoxicillin. They can expect the patient's symptoms to improve within three to four days and for the patient to be fully recovered with no symptoms at all in around ten days.

Complicated problems are those that have multiple factors and variables and may be unfamiliar yet still have a predictable and knowable cause-and-effect relationship. They can be considered simple problems with multiple steps because there is still a known rule or set of rules that will lead you to the solution. Implementing a new security software on every employee's computer or coordinating the ability for all employees to work remotely through the use of Zoom

---

* The right tool can make a difficult task easy, but the wrong tool can make an easy task difficult. My kids prefer this version: Using the wrong tool for the job is like trying to eat soup with a fork; you might make some progress, but it's going to be messy.

or other videoconferencing platforms can be a complicated problem. It requires careful planning, integration, project management, and coordination among multiple departments including IT, finance, and other teams. The solution is clear and achievable, but it demands a structured approach and multiple steps.

Complex and chaotic problems are "unordered," meaning cause and effect are unknown and can be deduced only with hindsight or not at all (unknowable).

Complex problems do not have clear cause-and-effect relationships. Cause and effect can only be deduced in retrospect, and thus, there are no clear right answers. Solutions are not apparent—in fact, the solution or answer only comes after the interaction of multiple elements, so it is unpredictable. For example, addressing performance issues on a team is a complex problem. Some of these causes may be easy to identify, while others may be hidden. There may be considerations that are consequences of other factors, much like the poor performance of one team member may be a consequence of their lack of skills, which itself is a consequence of the organization's recruitment and induction processes. Addressing a problem like this one may require trial and error, experimentation, learning as you go, and adaptation.

Finally, with chaotic problems, cause and effect is often unknowable. We not only struggle to define the problem but to grasp when it has actually been solved. It might even be impossible to definitively solve the problem. There may be no right or wrong universal solution, and right or wrong is only determined by the particulates at hand. Each problem is unique, so previous solutions to similar problems may not work in the current context. For example, for a company responding to a major cybersecurity breach, cause and effect are unclear. There are too many possible solutions to list and properly compare with each other, so the company might choose to isolate affected systems, deploy emergency security measures, and conduct a forensic investigation to understand the origin of the breach. But whether these measures will fully contain the breach and prevent further damage is not certain.

Known Knowns, Known Unknowns, and Unknown Unknowns

On February 12, 2002, former United States Secretary of Defense Donald Rumsfeld said:

> There are known knowns; there are things we know we know. We also know there are known unknowns; that is to say we know there are some things we do not know. But there are also unknown unknowns, the ones we don't know we don't know.

This may be one of the most profound quotes* I've ever encountered.

Known knowns are things we know we know. For example, facts. They represent the information and insights that we possess or that we can acquire, the foundation upon which we base our strategies and actions—for *simple problems*.

Known unknowns are the gaps in our knowledge or under-

---

* Profound because it illustrates the different levels of uncertainty and the challenges of dealing with unknowns. Its profundity, at least in my eyes, is separate from the original context of his words, which was connected to Iraq and weapons of mass destruction. The challenges of dealing with unknowns, particularly in complex situations like military planning, however, is profound.

standing that we are aware of. Known unknowns often prompt further exploration or investigation. We can address these through research or consultations with experts and employ strategies such as scenario planning, risk analysis, and contingency planning. Known unknowns speak to *complicated problems*.

Unknown unknowns represent what we don't know we don't know, the unforeseen and the unexpected. Unknown unknowns are the most challenging to address because they are outside of our awareness and may only become apparent later on. Unknown unknowns are *complex or chaotic problems*.

Situational Response

Simple, complicated, complex, and chaotic—each is a different kind of problem, yet we tend to approach all problems as if they are all the same.

Simple problems don't require our gut feel. All they require is for us to follow a rule or method.

Complicated problems should not involve our gut feel, even though the word *complicated* makes us think otherwise. We see a complicated problem and equate complication with difficulty. A complicated problem is not necessarily a difficult problem. What makes it complicated is that it may be "large" and there may be many parts to solve (which will certainly take hard work), it may be unfamiliar to you, or it may require more data or guidance—but it is solvable. Analytically solvable and deterministic. You might require certain expertise, training, or analysis—or you might need to find the right person or persons with that expertise. You might need to consult, do your research, and get help with some of the logical reasoning to solve the problem, but it is possible to work rationally toward a decision. Diagnosing a specific medical condition, designing a bridge, building a space shuttle—none of these should be based on gut feel because there are physiological systems, laws of physics, and tried and tested procedures that can help us arrive at an optimal "right" answer.

Let me say this another way. Our reason and logic alone are enough to solve simple or complicated problems. The intuiting process is unnecessary. At best, it's redundant, such as in those cases where your gut feel says the same thing that the hard data and analysis produced. At worst, it will contradict the hard data and lead us to the wrong solution. Think of a Rubik's Cube. You should never use your gut feel to solve a Rubik's Cube, which is ultimately just a series of simple problems. Is it difficult? Yes. Is it complicated? Absolutely. But it is fully solvable and actually straightforward when the method is deconstructed and unpacked. Most of us, however (me included), are reluctant to put in the work, so when we see a Rubik's Cube, we twist and rotate the cube, manipulating the colored squares "intuitively" to "solve" the puzzle. Those who try to solve a Rubik's Cube in earnest would never use their gut feel.

Our gut feel can be erroneous when solving simple and complicated problems. Again, this is perhaps why we've heard decision science scholars claim gut feel as "biased" or prone to heuristical* mistakes. One of the most common areas where we rely on gut feel and often get it wrong is routine hiring decisions; despite instincts about a candidate's fit, biases and first impressions can lead to overlooking crucial qualifications or potential red flags, resulting in costly mistakes. We similarly trust our gut instincts to predict straightforward market trends or time simple product launches or set prices

---

* *Heuristic + hysterical = heuristical.*

based on intuition rather than market research and cost analysis. We rely on gut feel during simple negotiations rather than on preparation and understanding the counterpart's position. We choose to enter into partnerships or collaborations based on a "good feeling" about the potential partner without thorough due diligence—which we accept is difficult, annoying, and complicated, so much so that we overlook that it's just a series of knowable steps.

We also make mistakes in the other direction—assessing a problem as simple or complicated when it is actually complex or chaotic. This is equally damaging. We tend to oversimplify, rely on "entrained thinking," whereby we apply erroneous data, frameworks, and pattern matching to situations that call for something entirely different that involves the more innovative, creative, and personal.* This happens when we might prioritize our projects at work simply based on deadlines and release dates because that's what is most logical and makes sense but fail to recognize that some of the stakeholders have their own priorities and fixations and part of our job is intuitively knowing how to keep certain people happy and in which ways.

Or we might approach a complex project launch based on data we received from customer focus groups. It seems like a simple problem—the data is literally telling us which features will be most successful—but there are all sorts of preferences and layers of complexity that we might not be accounting for. What makes this hard is that there is no system, no formula, no flowchart to tell us that *all* project launches or *all* hiring decisions are complex and chaotic or, conversely, simple. Some are simple because they can be broken

---

* This is not to say that data, frameworks, and pattern matching are not innovative or creative, just that intuition brings in that which is truly *personal* and *experiential* to give color and meaning to what might otherwise be "just" innovative or creative.

down into solvable pieces; some are anything but simple because there are unknowable contingencies.

One reason Taylor Swift is breaking records is because of her bold and brilliant move from country to pop—she tuned into her intuition and took what many would have assessed as simple and recognized it as complex and chaotic. All the customer data was telling her the "right" way to continue capitalizing on her devoted audience. But instead, she saw that it was more complicated than that. Leading up to her *1989* album, she wrote, "For the last few years, I've woken up every day not wanting, but *needing* to write a new style of music. . . . I needed to change the way I told my stories and the way they sounded. . . . It was a good thing to follow this gut feeling."

In an interview with the *Montreal Gazette*, she elaborated, "I had this constant intuition and gut feeling and inspiration coming at me saying: 'Make this album this way, make this album different from everything you've done before.' So creatively I just followed that intuition and made the album the way I wanted to make it." And even when her record label worried about offending all the country radio stations that had supported her work over the years, and asked her to include three country songs on *1989*, she politely declined because she knew that she had to make a clean break.

It is for such types of complex and chaotic problems that we need our schemas, mental models, and prototypes. It is in these situations that trusting our intuition will serve us best. We need to bring *together* both the external data and our personal experience. When we remember and adhere to this, our intuition never steers us wrong. This sounds like a platitude, but only because truth, accuracy, omniscience, and infallibility are complicated philosophical distinctions. Some might ask: If it's true that our culminating gut feel never lies, then why are chaotic problems like climate change or geopolitical wars still unresolved? Can't we just task those solving these problems to rely on their intuition? Our gut feel never lies, but it's not omniscient. Our gut feel will always tell us the truth, but that doesn't mean that it's always "right," because life will always have contingencies, exceptions, and distinctions that we must account for in the intuiting process.

In other words: You won't win every poker hand, but at the end of the night, you'll finish in the money overall. It's specifically for this reason that we have to hone and develop our gut feel, so that it is more right than wrong. If we're using it as a tool, then we have to sharpen it, so it serves us best in the right contexts.

Solving complex and chaotic problems requires a deep understanding of the problem itself as well as your unique role in the problem based on your lived experiences, your priors. It necessitates a multifaceted strategy, which is fine-tuned as it is implemented— one that can only be accomplished by going beyond pure rational, hard data to include all the patterns, schemas, and mental models that you've harnessed along the way.

If data and analysis are available and applicable, then rely on those. If you can calculate the probability of the outcome with reasonable confidence, don't use gut feel. But for problems like reducing traffic congestion in a city, contending with natural disasters, navigating sociopolitical challenges, addressing global issues like climate change and pandemics—these are complex, chaotic situations where the outcomes are unpredictable, and the solutions require the breadth of personal experience, data analysis, experimentation, and adaptation over time. So, too, are complex workplace decisions that we have to make with regard to hiring, firing, product development, purchasing, customer service, competition, investments, mergers and acquisitions, growth and expansion, and so on—when we can't be sure of the outcome. We need data plus experience to navigate these situations more fluidly and gracefully.

Why do some of these problems seem simple (or straightforward, at least) when they are actually complex? How can we tell the difference? Peter Bloch, Frederic Brunel, and Todd Arnold, researchers seeking to understand product aesthetics, for example, studied product purchasing decisions and found that the complexity of the visual aesthetics alone—physical design attributes such as color, texture, and shape—was enough to create an infinite number of iterations that would confound decision makers. Add intangible aesthetic properties such as harmony, pliability, musicality, responsibility, and situational normality, and decisions such as these were truly chaotic. There will always be unknowns.

In other cases, perhaps there are some factors that are knowable, but others that are not. When deciding to launch a new product, you'd likely do research on the addressable market and competitor products, but your analysis will not guarantee that people will buy the product. When deciding to divest a business, you will likely look at models, figures, and forecasts, but there will be huge uncertainties and many factors—product portfolio, organizational culture, ongoing operations, to name a few—that will still be unknowable.

Complex problems and chaotic problems can be broken down into pieces that are actually simple or "just" complicated. Certainly, we can get data and analyze those pieces systematically, but what makes these problems ultimately complex or chaotic is that there are key parts that are unknowable, so we must rely on and apply our gut feel.

How to solve . . .

Simple problems	Be aware. Identify the rule. Employ the rule. Don't overthink.
Complicated problems	Be strategic. Break it down into a series of simpler problems. Solve each simple problem. Add more people (experts) to help with each simple problem, if needed.
Complex problems	Be reflective. Recognize that there are too many possible solutions to list and properly compare with each other in a rational manner. Separate problems from symptoms. **Rely on your gut feel.**
Chaotic problems	Be tacit. Recognize that there are multiple dynamics and no clear right or wrong solutions. **Rely on your gut feel.**

5

Gut Feel Compels Action (and Re-Action)

*Putting your gut feel into action is about bold
strokes (the spark of inspiration) as well
as long marches (the journey toward
realization and resolution).*

I n March 2007, Cynthia Carroll became the chief executive of Anglo American, a mining conglomerate that is responsible for about 40 percent of the world's output of platinum and diamonds—it owns an 85 percent share of De Beers—and is also a major producer of copper, nickel, iron ore, and coal. It employs over ninety-five thousand permanent employees and thirty thousand contract employees, with two-thirds of the company based in South Africa. Carroll was the first non–South African and the first female chief executive of Anglo American.

Three months after assuming leadership, Carroll was flying from the company's platinum mines in Rustenburg, South Africa, to Johannesburg, when chief executive of Anglo American Platinum, Ralph Havenstein, pulled her aside and said: "We've had another fatality." That brought the total number of fatalities in that year alone to twenty-nine miners.

Carroll felt a deep, sudden jolt. With one bold stroke, she turned to Havenstein and said: "We're closing the mines."

She knew her decision would affect jobs—closing operations would result in the displacement of over thirty thousand workers, most of whom were the sole breadwinners for their families. She'd have to figure out whether they would keep paying workers while the mines were closed.

Carroll anticipated that there would be reverberations within affected local communities. Closing the mines would lead to a huge negative impact, both economically and socially in these communities, including increased poverty due to the reduced business activity.

She understood that there would be substantial financial losses to the company itself—in addition to losses in revenue, they would have to write off assets and cover numerous costs, including site rehabilitation expenses. In sum, it would amount to more than $8 million in losses *per day* while Rustenburg was closed. She would have a lot of explaining to do to shareholders and the board of Anglo American.

She realized that these financial losses would create additional economic ripples that would have massive, international, industry-wide impact—suppliers, contractors, and other businesses that rely on the mining operation would also suffer huge financial setbacks or closures due to reduced trickle-down demand for their services. The company's reputation and relationships would be affected. There would be strained relationships with other stakeholders, including employees, local communities, investors, and regulators. Finally, Carroll was acutely aware of her own obligation to the company, the local government, other executives, superintendents, site managers, and miners—the obligations that she had taken on when she agreed to lead this company.

Yet, despite all of these, Cynthia Carroll didn't hesitate. As soon as she heard that there was another death, it was as if she'd received a new piece information that took her to a different level of consciousness. There was a split-second moment of pause, and then that pause turned to action.

Carroll closed the Rustenburg Mining Complex, saying, "I simply cannot support operations that are killing people." Members of her team suggested waiting until the next morning to make the decision, to which she immediately replied, "Start bringing people up from the ground *now*." She closed all nine shafts of the mine, and instructed that all workers be paid during the closure. She set the following conditions to reopening the Rustenburg mines: They must first get input from every single worker on issues at the mines, and all of the mines must be in full compliance with Anglo American Platinum's safety standards.

To accomplish this, on day one, workers were told that management wanted to hear from them and that safety was Anglo American's number one priority. Given the complex history of South Africa, which was marked by centuries of migration and colonization and decades of apartheid, leading to divisions among various groups each with their own distinct languages, cultures, and affiliations, Carroll knew she had to go beyond typical methods of corporate communications. She had industrial theater groups perform, showing workers speaking out. She also put employees into groups of forty to fifty and, using lekgotla, a traditional South African method of conducting village assemblies, enabled them to voice their concerns to supervisors in a manner they were familiar with that gave them psychological safety.

On days two through five, they started the work of bringing the shafts up to safety standards, while all workers were retrained. Anglo American executives were flown in from around the world to help. It took weeks before the mines reopened, and the closure resulted in $40 million in losses.

Carroll continued taking action, and more action based on those re-actions. In February 2008, Anglo American introduced the 10 Fatal Risk Standards, based on worldwide best practices. Two months later, Carroll held the first Tripartite Safety Summit, convening individuals from Anglo American, the National Union of Mineworkers, and the South African government. She followed up this summit with a series of world tours, with people from all three stakeholders, paid for by Anglo American, to study safety best practices. These summits continued on a quarterly basis, and the Solidarity Union said: "We work together today in a way that was inconceivable before Cynthia. . . . The tripartite created a new standard by which relationships between the unions, government, and business are now judged in South Africa."

In November 2008, Anglo American introduced its first ever set of Guiding Values, including a focus on safety and "Care and Respect" for all employees. Throughout that year, Anglo American executives were trained in the new Safety Risk Management Programme, and every Anglo American department was required to formulate a safety plan, with bonuses partly dependent on it. In addition, the bonuses of all Anglo American executives, including Carroll, were determined in part by how many interactions they had with frontline workers. Memorials were held across Anglo American for any worker killed—and their supervisors were required to visit the worker's home village, in person, to offer their condolences.

Anglo American also began to develop new technologies to improve safety, and shared these technologies with the entire industry, including their competitors.

Under Carroll's leadership, fatalities dropped from twenty-nine to thirteen, and the injury rate dropped by almost 50 percent. Despite Carroll never getting to her goal of "Zero Harm" by the time she stepped down in April 2013 and productivity never improving to pre-shutdown levels at Rustenburg, the mining industry still refers to two periods of safety: "pre-Cynthia" and "post-Cynthia." Carroll changed the way the mining industry thinks about safety, and Chris Griffith, Head of Anglo American Platinum, stated, "Perhaps we would have more production if we were not so focused on safety. But who wants to be part of a leadership team that's destroying things everywhere they go? I would much rather be a leader known for making a little less money but sending home sixty thousand people safely to their families at the end of each work day. . . . This is what society expects of us, this is what we expect of ourselves."

Bold Strokes and Long Marches

Bold strokes are major actions that we take. They disrupt our taken-for-granted, day-to-day routines. For Carroll, her bold stroke—immediately closing the mines—sent a signal to the rest of the organization. It commanded attention. Rick Cohen, in his decision to move to self-managed teams—all in, right away, rather than doing it gradually or waiting until after the holidays—also made a bold stroke. Bold strokes are one's gut feel.

But just as we discussed how gut feel is the conclusive endpoint to a (long) intuiting process, there is a process that follows a gut feel breakthrough: long marches of sustained programs that must accompany and follow bold strokes. In John Kotter's work, he outlines a model for successful organizational transformation and describes how significant change often requires bold initiatives to create a sense of urgency and momentum, complemented by sustained efforts to embed new practices and behaviors into the organizational culture. They are what make our gut feel not *just* about making the "right decision" but also about the actions that create the durable conditions to support your gut feel.

Bold Strokes	Long Marches
• Major actions or moves that disrupt the taken-for-granted, day-to-day routine.	• Sustained programs of change to an individual's, team's, or organization's hardware and software.
• Often send a signal to yourself (and others). They command attention.	• Create durable conditions to support your gut feel and help you (and others) see how changes will eventually become the new taken-for-granted way of doing things.

This is an important point because what actually makes a decision the "right decision"? It's not *just* having a gut feel that results in closing the mines, as was the case with Cynthia Carroll. It's that Carroll made a choice *and* set out to make it work. Throughout the long march, there were times that she had to fix things, re-act, make pivots, course-correct, completely revamp, and try something new. Knowing that all of this was likely was part of the information that Carroll considered during the intuiting process—which led to her decision to close the mines, what I call the gut feel decision—and part of what made it *the* right decision. As I tell my kids often, trust your gut feel, make a decision, take action, and continue to fix things. Or, as Ralph Waldo Emerson said more eloquently, "A gut feeling is like a compass in the wilderness; it guides you through uncharted territory, but it's your actions that turn it into a path."

Making Sense of Paradox

Let's start with a deeper dive into the action behind the bold strokes. Afterward, we'll explore the series of actions behind the long march, the re-actions.

The bold stroke is required of us because the hallmark of *any* crisis or substantive problem that we are facing—any complex or chaotic situation—is ambiguity. We lack crucial information, but we still need to make good decisions, so we need to be attuned to what our gut feel is telling us about our priors and the prompts.

Journalist and author Napoleon Hill once conducted an analysis of several hundred people who had accumulated fortunes (including Andrew Carnegie, Henry Ford, and Charles Schwab), and found that every one of them had a habit of reaching decisions quickly. They were decisive.

Successful people make decisions quickly and firmly. They make fast decisions and move forward knowing that, at best, 70 percent of their decisions are going to be right. They move the ball forward every day. They are quick to spot their mistakes and then course-correct as needed. They do this by (quickly) making sense of paradox.

We face paradoxes in our lives all the time: The early bird gets the worm. The second mouse gets the cheese. Birds of a feather flock together. Opposites attract. The pen is mightier than the sword. Actions speak louder than words.

These are my favorites:

The more you know, the less you understand.

—LAO TZU

The only constant in life is change.

—HERACLITUS

We face situations in our lives that similarly appear to be self-contradictory or logically inconsistent—complex, if you will. For example, the work-life balance paradox so widely discussed that we no longer even believe there to be a "real" solution. We strive to excel in our careers, but to do so may require long hours, dedication, and hard work—which can lead to burnout, strained relationships, and neglect of personal health and well-being. We want career advancement, financial security, and a sense of accomplishment, but we also want to enjoy life outside of work.

In the workplace, do we innovate to stay competitive or maintain stability in your current operations? Innovation can lead to breakthrough products that capture new markets and generate revenue growth, but innovation is costly and risky, and often disrupts existing processes and require substantial investment that needs to come from existing business. Do we provide employees with autonomy or maintain control? Striking the right balance between empowering employees with decision-making authority, while also maintaining necessary levels of oversight is not easy. Centralize or decentralize? Risk-taking or risk aversion? Buy or sell?

What is it that allows us to take that bold stroke of action when confronted with any of these paradoxes? What is it that allows us to make that leap?

A state of focused abstraction.

It's Not What You Look At; It's What You See

Focused abstraction is a state in which we've selectively filtered and simplified information to extract essential elements or patterns while disregarding all other irrelevant details. It allows us to comprehend complexity or uncertainty by concentrating on specific aspects that are most salient and relevant. It's like finally seeing the Magic Eye object.

In the 1990s, there was an op art phenomenon that briefly took over the world: Magic Eye posters. Magic Eye was a shape hiding in the midst of a graphic mess of autostereogram grids, hypercolored patterns, and random dots and dashes. People would swear by all sorts of techniques: *Just look through the paper. Don't cross your eyes. Try to squint and then relax.* At some point, you'd see it. The image would appear, and then you wouldn't be able to unsee it. All the

Magic Eye Autostereograms

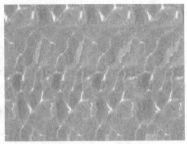

peripheral information somehow became irrelevant, and all other parts of the picture were distilled into that one image. When we arrive at this state, we have focused abstraction. Everything is "centered" for us, and it doesn't matter what anyone else thinks, because you see the key or crown or flower. (The coolest one that I've ever seen is a great white shark swimming.) Everything else is just noise. When everyone else sees the Ys in $YYYYXYYYY$, but you notice the X, that's all that matters. You're able to focus on what the X means and take quick action.

When we experience Eureka, Spidey Sense, or Jolt, something has happened, or some new information has been provided, that allows us to abstract and focus quickly, often subliminally, to diagnose the problem. It brings us to a different level of consciousness and we see the problem in a new light. As Albert Einstein once said, "We cannot solve our problems with the same thinking we used when we created them." That new thinking, or that new perspective, is what gives us that aha feeling and spurs us to action.

Put simply, focused abstraction is the mechanism that links our gut feel breakthrough (a thought) and the bold stroke (an action).

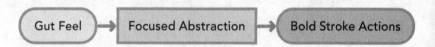

Dan Giusti, the chef who left Noma, is a perfect example of this. His gut feel resulted in an intense abstracting and focusing mechanism, where his attention and concentration was brought to a specific aspect, detail, or task. His mind was brought back to his aunt's tomato sauce, to memories of her feeding many people every day. It helped him understand what he had been feeling but hadn't been able to place for months. Food for all, delicious food for everyone—no matter who you were—to enjoy. He grew up understanding this, but he had not been able to see it until that moment.

A few months later, Dan founded Brigaid, a company revolutionizing institutional food service programs, bringing professional chefs and culinary expertise at the service of kids in school cafeterias, incarcerated people in prisons, and sick people in hospitals—food for all.

Similarly, it was also only by getting to a state of focused abstraction that Diana, a public city official, was able to see the emergence of the right solution to reduce traffic congestion in a city. When I interviewed her, she was living in a city that faced a chaotic problem involving road infrastructure, public transportation, commuting patterns, urban planning, and more. The problem was continuing to grow and there was a sense of urgency in solving it, but for months, Diana didn't know how. She and her team had already tried all sorts of things to manage congestion. They had implemented congestion pricing, where vehicles are charged a fee to enter certain congested areas, thereby encouraging people to use public transportation or travel less. They also offered reduced fares, subsidies, and tax breaks to encourage people to use public transportation. Nothing seemed to have an impact.

Driving into work[*] one day, however, she saw the equivalent of her Magic Eye object: She recognized that improvements to mass transit, carpooling, and ride-sharing wouldn't fix the problem of congestion, as they had been discussing for months. It wasn't about reducing congestion at all—it was about *spreading* the congestion

---

[*] As one of the only public city officials who commuted each day on the central highway through the city, Diana understood many things that others did not, which allowed her to "see it."

by managing travel times and travel patterns, which in turn would naturally take care of crowding. She was only brought to a state of focused abstraction that allowed her to have this Eureka because her abnormal meeting schedule that week found her driving into work at different times of day than she usually did. There was no congestion, and any fees she was paying to enter those areas were irrelevant. This made her realize that they were going about it in the wrong way. It wasn't just about reducing congestion itself. Instead, it was about managing patterns of travel—which involved working with local businesses to understand their telecommuting options and flexible work hours (perhaps offering *them* incentives) so that people could drive to work at different times of day, thereby managing the flow of people commuting during peak traffic times.

Starve Your Distractions, Feed Your Focus

Focused abstraction directs your mental energy and capacities to a particular problem or goal, allowing you to critically filter out distractions or peripheral and irrelevant information. You're then able to draw from your mental models, schemas, memories, and experiences to act. You don't worry about the risks and concerns that you had when you were in the midst of problem-solving. You just act and continue to take steps along the long march.

It's during the long march that the wisdom of one of my students kicks in. As I was interviewing him, he keenly stated, "I feel like I start with my gut feel, and then check it (with data). That whole thing is my gut feel, if that makes sense."

It made sense to me completely. Data is meant to enhance intuition. It's integrated into both the early introspection before and the actions during the long march. Simply put, it's during the bold stroke that we act in spite of the risk. It's during the long march that we work to make the risk irrelevant. We can manage the risk because we've attained a level of consciousness that gives us a new perspective on the risk. For Dan Giusti, the long march was how to make Brigaid a success—all the steps he'd need to take to build this new business that catered to schoolkids, the incarcerated, and the sick. The voice that asked, "What will people say about me not being chef at Noma?" or "What will I do?" became irrelevant.

I saw this in the investors I interviewed for my PhD research. When they were making decisions to invest in early-stage start-ups, they emphasized that gut feel was *the* factor that emboldened them to make investments that would otherwise be considered overly risky and likely to lead to failure (99.9 percent of early-stage start-ups never achieve profitability). That was their bold stroke. What they called their gut feel provided them with a mechanism for "cognitively and emotionally reframing investment risk into a compelling narrative that transcends avoidance behavior," per my dissertation. In other words: Gut feel was almost an *excuse*—a great excuse—for making what others would deem an irrationally risky decision). They could think in terms of a portfolio strategy (1 successful investment at a 30x return more than makes up for 25 complete losses) so that the risk of each individual "mistake" is seemingly irrelevant—but then make their investment decision a wise one by taking all the steps required during the long march (mentoring, making introductions, assisting with strategy and operations) to ensure that their decision was ultimately the right one.

The process of achieving a state of focused abstraction is what helps us distinguish our gut feel from louder rational arguments. An investor I spoke with long after my dissertation had been completed validated this idea. It was 2019, and he was considering investing in a start-up called TravelBank, which had built a revolutionary on-line platform that allowed employees of large corporations to seamlessly book travel and directly generate expense reports. The start-up had enjoyed huge initial success in Q4 2019, but by May 2020, TravelBank had gone massively off course, dropping from $100 million in annual travel bookings to nearly nothing. This was unsurprising given that COVID-19 had wreaked havoc on travel across the world.

Worse, the funding promised by a number of investors pre-COVID was still outstanding. Venture capitalists were reneging on their commitments, and they all had the legal right to do so. Surprisingly, Carey Lai, one of the managing directors of venture capital firm Conductive Ventures and the investor whom I spoke with, decided to invest in the company at this exact point in time. Why? He said that he'd noticed something—that he was almost brought to a different dimension of understanding—about the opportunity, about the founding team, about the diamond in the rough that others were missing out on. His understanding of the company—what he previously believed about the industry, as well as what all other existing investors believed—was that there would indeed be havoc in the travel industry because of COVID. But for Carey, he had a profound sense that there was something that other investors were not seeing. TravelBank was not a travel company at all. It was an expense management company. Instead of selling travel, they should be selling expense management.

Carey wired over the money. And then he got to work, taking small actions to help TravelBank pivot to the expense management market. Together, they continued to make quick, major adjustments to TravelBank's product offering and revenue model so that it could not only survive but thrive. In July 2021, TravelBank was acquired by US Bancorp for an amount estimated at around $200 million.

How do we achieve a state of focused abstraction, just like Carey did? We'll learn how in part II.

PART II

Intentional Intuition

Give me six hours to chop down a tree, and I will spend the first four sharpening the axe.

ABRAHAM LINCOLN

6

Perceptible: How Do I Engage My Intuition?

We can take our gut feel from the passive to the active. We can learn how to intentionally engage our intuiting process so it's perceptible, to help solve our greatest problems.

The Stone Journey. Lee Mingwei (b. 1964), 李明維. Stone and bronze. Height: 5.5 cm. (2 1/4 in.). Width: 3.7 cm. (1 1/2 in.). Depth: 2.0 cm. (7/8 in.). Mounted on wood. Description: *Two rocks. One, an exquisite mineral that was thrown up by the earth approximately 70 million years ago. The other, a bronze replica cast that is indistinguishable in terms of size, weight, or any other discernible feature. Together, these rocks comprise Lee Mingwei's* The Stone Journey.

W hich would you throw out?" asked my friend Cesar as he pointed at the stones.

"I beg your pardon?" I stuttered, completely caught off guard.

Cesar repeated his question, but gave me a bit more context this time: The stone (one of them, at least) was found in the Porporai

River Valley, an area carved out and shaped by glacial movement seventy million years ago, in what is now New Zealand's South Island. *That* stone is considered a wonder of nature, he remarked. It was discovered in the riverbeds of the valley as a glacial artifact and, when held in the palm of your hands, is said to feel unusually cool and soothing. The second stone, he explained, was the replica made of bronze.

Upon acquiring this piece of art, the artist Lee Mingwei places an obligation on the owner: They must decide which stone to keep. The other must be discarded. What is curious and cleverly adroit about this piece of work is that there is a problem being posed to the owner, along with a call to action.

At first glance, the problem seems simple: Figure out which is the natural stone and which is the replica. What information might help us distinguish between the two?

We quickly realize that it might be a complicated problem. You could frame the question as "Which do you throw out?" or "Which do you keep?"

Simply by recognizing that there are two ways in which we could frame the question, I understood that beyond the decision of which is "real" and which is "fake," I had the agency to decide whether to, in fact, comply with the artist's obligation. Must we actually throw one away? If so, when? When does this obligation come due?

The decision becomes more complex. We're confronted with the notion of ownership. What does it mean to own something? The owner of the art may find himself or herself unable to part with either stone, in which case, can they pass that decision along to their heirs? We're confronted with the concept of value. Which stone is actually more precious, the natural one or the replica? Ordinarily, in the art world, the original would be more valuable than a copy. But is that true in this case? Which is more desirable, and hence worth more? We're confronted with the concept of self and intimacy. Which is more desirable to me?

You realize that there's something more complex, chaotic, even, when you see and appreciate that all of this might not even be about the rocks themselves. They become symbolic of something much bigger—like time, and how it is central to this process and every process in life, and control, the artist's as well as ours. Life, like the questions this piece of art raises, is an open-ended scenario.

Lee Mingwei once noted that we must consider that over time, one or both stones might be lost unintentionally—to children's play, accident, destruction—and the decision would then have been made by forces beyond the owner's control. What might the owner feel about such an event: loss, relief, disappointment, resignation?

There are so many possibilities and consequences that the artist invites us—forces us—to consider. As Lee Mingwei says, this piece "expands the limits of our aesthetic consciousness."

Your Focus Determines Your Reality

Which would *you* throw out? What *The Stone Journey* represents is how we can take a complex, chaotic, even impenetrable problem but still *solve it* by activating our gut feel. We might have an initial impulse about which stone is the "real" stone. But there is a much longer intuiting process that we can purposely and intentionally lead ourselves through in the journey, as we move from a passive stance to an active one.

There is no way to solve the conundrum of *The Stone Journey* without *you* because the decision depends on you and what you value. What Lee Mingwei calls aesthetic consciousness is, in essence, just a fancy way of saying gut feel—and it has to be *your* gut feel. Based on your priors, you have to know who you are, what you value, what is most desirable to you, and what your obligation is. On this complex, potentially chaotic problem, rely on your intuition to come up with the answer.

In actuality, this piece of art isn't about throwing anything out. Even if you never do anything with either stone, the thought exercise makes salient to us that our gut feel has the potential to provide us with incredible capacities for solving problems. It's like a compass and as long as we understand how it works and we continue to sharpen it, tune it, and regulate it, it'll guide us in the right direction.

Most books about intuition or gut feel stop at the *passive*—the equivalent of telling you that you have a compass to help you navigate—without providing you with the knowledge to train your gut feel to be *active*.

Let's start with **introspection**, which ties into the first insight we uncovered in part I of the book, which is that gut feel is *you*. Introspection is our ability to be in touch with our priors. Though we are starting with introspection, which temporally occurs at the outset of the intuiting process, I will continue to refer to and highlight gut feel because we can only see and understand the intuiting process in relation to the outcome that we're aiming toward. Like in archery, always being attuned to the characteristics of the target—its position, size, and distance—is crucial because it informs every aspect of your practice, from mastering your stance and grip to refining your aim and release, ultimately guiding the strategies and techniques you employ to consistently hit the mark with precision.

Digging deeper, we'll see that introspection is the process of looking inward, in an even more structured manner, to make sense of ourselves vis-à-vis our traits and characteristics and to become aware of how we physically embody the signals that we're sending to ourselves. We'll also examine our emotions, as well as the schemas, mental models, and prototypes we've constructed for ourselves based on our lived experiences. We'll discuss thought exercises, applied tips, and methods of practice. For example, we might write down three things that we are grateful for before going to bed each night, or we might get into the habit each morning of documenting any dreams or nightmares that we might remember from the night before. These exercises will help us further hone our understanding and our ability to engage in introspection.

After introspection, which concerns our priors, we'll study the *interactions* that occur between prompts and our priors to produce our gut feel. This will help us recognize how our *own* Eureka, Spidey Sense, and Jolts might present and manifest. Improving our sensitivity to inputs, becoming more intentional about observing what we might previously have ignored, and making sense of these prompts help us get to a state of focused abstraction that compels action. We'll cover exercises and practical activities to help us more fully comprehend these interactions.

Finally, we'll develop and harness the power of *iterations*, understanding that although gut feel doesn't lie, it can be misinterpreted during the intuiting process. We can learn from our experiences that led us to situational arrogance and mistakes. We can draw on these past failures to inform and refine our entire intuiting process. Suggested exercises will help make these lessons more concrete.

What makes our gut feel a superpower is our ability to go from the passive to the active. We can move beyond self-awareness and become intentionally attuned to our priors, so that we can activate them in response to a prompt, rather than have them remain buried and dormant.

For instance, take the dozens of people I interviewed who talked about using their gut feel during job searches and career uncertainties. If we put ourselves in their places for a moment, we can all imagine considering a job offer that we may have just received. As you are talking with people about the offer and getting advice, suddenly, something doesn't quite feel right. You can't put your finger on it, but you have a sense of discomfort. Despite your impressive qualifications, your fit for the position, and all the positive aspects of the company and the role, you can't shake off the feeling of unease. You end up not taking the job because you trust your gut feel. But that feeling was never translated into an active state of understanding—it was never diagnosed—and as a result, you often think back, wondering if you should have taken it, or perhaps, at moments when you are unhappy or feel unsuitable in subsequent roles, you regret that you didn't accept that particular offer.

Alternatively, let's say that after suddenly feeling that something isn't quite right, you discern that you are having a Spidey Sense about something related to that company. You engage with this sensation, find a quiet space, close your eyes, and take deep breaths to center yourself. You think about what prompted the Spidey Sense: Was there a prompt that was misaligned with your priors? What is it that is actually bothering you? You realize that what is bugging you is something that is entirely, seemingly, tangential: Your son was upset last night after his soccer game. What? Totally out of left field, you think to yourself. Except that it's not. You reflect on the last interview you had with the woman who would be your director at this company. Because you had sharpened your ability to listen and interpret prompts, you recall that she seemed to focus on how her team and the company are "her family." It had made you think about your own family, and though she had continued to position the "company as a family" as an asset—as a culture of supportiveness, positivity, and closeness—you recognized it as dependency, unrealistic demands, and enmeshment, where there would be an expectation of unconditional loyalty and a culture of alienation for those who did not fit the perceived "family" mold. The prompt (our company is like a "family") and your priors (your son, family, values) were in dissonance.

You continue to consider your priors and prompts and what you value, and you bring yourself to a state of focused abstraction. You filter, intentionally probe, and uncover a deeper insight into why this opportunity does not align with your aspirations. As a result, you reject this offer, and you take steps to narrow your future search, refine how you engage in interviews going forward, and ultimately find a job that isn't perfect, but is fulfilling and purposeful. It becomes the springboard that allows you to take the next job a few years later, and then the next suitable one, in your long marches.

This is the difference between passive and active. Centered within this difference is the honing and harnessing and sharpening of your intuition. When you actively engage your gut feel it has the potential to give you profound, almost superhuman-like powers of problem-solving. It's like how we are told to "engage your core" when exercising. When we engage our core, we are activating and contracting the muscles in our abdomen, lower back, and pelvis to stabilize our spine. When we learn to engage our core, we enhance our performance to levels we didn't think possible, make continuous improvements to our posture, stability, and overall strength, and tremendously reduce the risk of injury in physical tasks. Engaging our gut feel is no different. Mastering our intuition is like noticing, working out, and defining our muscles.

Passive gut feel is based on spontaneous intuitive insights that something might not align with our values or expectations, without us being able to pinpoint the exact reason. This feeling is a message we get, like a whisper from within, offering subtle nudges and inclinations that can guide our decisions. Active gut feel is investigating that message deliberately and intentionally, which enables us to access deeper insights.

Mastering Your Intuition

Exercise: Understand your baseline tendency toward
passivity versus activity in using your gut feel.

If you had to rate yourself on a scale of 0 (*I just go with my gut*; passive gut feel) to 100 (*I investigate what my gut feel is telling me and go with the deeper insights I discover*; active gut feel), what number would you give yourself? Where would you say you fall on the scale?

Baseline Tendency Toward Active Gut Feel

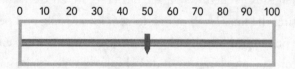

If you're not sure (if you don't have a gut feel about it), consider some of these scenarios. These are not perfect indicators because they are highly context dependent, so rather than using this is as an evaluation tool, think of it more as a reflective provocation that might help you.

You're in a team meeting discussing a new project proposal. You feel a strong intuition that the project has potential for success. Are you more likely to:

A. Express your enthusiasm and support for moving forward.

B. Pay attention to your initial reaction, and notice that you have feelings of excitement and enthusiasm, but also pride, and that your reasons for wanting to move forward have to do with the potential rewards and desire to overcome challenging parts of the project.

You're faced with conflicting advice from colleagues about how to approach a problem at work. Are you more likely to:

A. Trust your intuition to guide you toward the best course of action, based on what feels right.

B. Actively engage your gut feel by noticing any feelings of resonance or discomfort that arise as you consider the different perspectives, while making a decision that aligns with your inner sense of the conflicting advice.

You're considering whether to speak up in a meeting about a concern you have regarding a proposed plan. Are you more likely to:

A. Feel a strong intuition that your input is valuable and speak up confidently based on your gut feel about the issue.

B. Pay attention to your inner sense of urgency regarding the issue, and focus your remarks on the significance of your concern and the potential impact of voicing it.

If you answered all three questions with an A, then you are likely in the 0–30 range. If you answered two questions with an A, you are likely in the 30–50 range; and if you answered just one question with an A, then the 50–70 range. If all responses were a B, then you're in the 70–100 range. These are all ranges because where you fall exactly, and what that means, is something that we'll continue to explore in the chapters to come. If you scored in the bottom 50 range (and I'd venture that most of us are below 50 on this scale), fret not, as all we are establishing at this point is that taking a passive versus active *stance* on a problem is different from tending toward a passive versus active *gut feel*.

Passivity involves not wanting to actively engage or take action. It's the extent to which we might avoid making decisions, stay within the bounds of nonactive intuiting, prefer to defer responsibility to others, or simply allow events to unfold without intervention. Passive gut feel, on the other hand, means that even though you might take action, you rely on instinctual responses without active questioning or evaluation.

Similarly, activity is about engaging, taking initiative, and exerting effort to address a situation or achieve a desired outcome, whereas active gut feel entails doing these while consciously engaging and reflecting on one's intuition as part of the decision-making or action-taking process.

We might have broad ranges of differences in terms of our propensity for passivity versus activity, but most of us (at least to start with) will find that we're low on the scale in terms of passive versus active gut feel. Just knowing and understanding this will allow you to begin to train your intuiting process.

I think of this notion of training sometimes when I'm trying to navigate a new city because I have a horrible sense of direction. If you say, "And then turn right at the ice cream shop," I'm the person who will have no recollection that I even passed an ice cream shop.

Recently, I was in Central Park in New York, getting some exercise during a forty-five-minute break at a conference I was attending. I was trying to not get lost so that I could make it back in time. I started by acknowledging that my natural propensity is to not pay attention. That made me more intentional. I made note that I did not go under that bridge, but I turned right instead. So on my way back, I'm going to pass that bridge and turn left. Yes, I remember that hot dog and pretzel vendor. I notice the chess and checkers tables so that when I retrace my steps, I'll recognize that I'm on the right track.

Knowing our tendency toward passivity versus activity allows us to think more intentionally when using our intuition and gut feel. Just as we navigate a new city by noticing landmarks and geographical points, we learn how to activate our gut feel by engaging in additional introspection on its personified, embodied, emotional, and cognitive dimensions, each of which we will be examining next.

Introspection

7

Personified: How Do I Describe Myself?

Our personified gut feel is honed when we have a self-awareness of our baseline traits and characteristics.

It's not often that Ariana Grande and the Dalai Lama are mentioned in the same sentence. Ariana Grande is prone to say things like "That time I dropped my groceries, had a bowl of Cheerios, and fell in love with my neighbor through the wall telepathically," whereas the Dalai Lama would say, "Whether or not we follow any particular spiritual tradition the benefits of love and kindness are obvious to anyone."

In 2019, together with a group of colleagues and researchers, I helped develop a measure called *forward flow*. Essentially, forward flow captures the steady flow of thoughts that passes through our brains and defines our mental life. It's like our stream of consciousness.

What we found is that a lot of the thinking that we engage in is about sensing relationships and making connections in our mind. And forward flow not only helps gauge one's tendency toward divergent or creative thought but exercising this tendency hones the muscles we use for focused abstraction.

Here's one way we measured it: Let's say I give you one word, *bear*. Write down the first word you think of after hearing *bear* (maybe it's *honey*). Then write down the next word you think of from *honey*, and so on.

Want to try it out before I tell you more? Your seed word is *toaster*.

_____

_____

_____

_____

_____

_____

_____

_____

_____

_____

_____

How do you think you did?* We studied thousands of individuals in various professions (actors, accountants, entrepreneurs, and so on) and had them do this simple exercise. Through this, we were able to measure their propensity for divergent thought.

While convergent thinking is associated with clear, well-defined parameters, where you are trying to reach a definitive conclusion or solution that is aligned with specific guidelines, divergent thinking involves generating multiple possibilities, ideas, or solutions that entails open-ended explorations of possibilities. Both types of thinking are valuable and can be applied in different contexts, depending on the nature of the problem or task at hand.

We determined the forward flow score by computing the semantic distance between two words—how far or close they are in meaning. For example, *snow* and *white* have a small semantic distance (they are close in meaning), whereas *snow* and *carburetor* have a large semantic distance.

In this graph, the lines in dark and light gray represent different individuals, each with a unique "thought plot." We can observe both the semantic distance between words and the semantic distance between the seed word (*toaster*) and the final word (*men* vs. *cake*). The individual in dark gray had a higher forward flow score and was rated as more creative (and able to see more relationships and connections) than the individual in light gray.

---

* You can score yourself, as well as read more about our custom LSA engine, at http://www.forwardflow.org.

Forward Flow Plots for Two Individuals

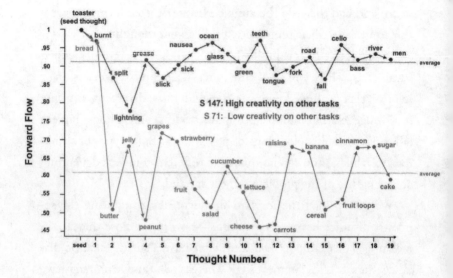

We also looked at celebrities, specifically, those who are "expected" to be creative in their life's vocation, versus those who are expected to be grounded and spiritual, for example, and found the predictive power of forward flow. We analyzed each of the one hundred most-followed X (formerly Twitter) users, including Jimmy Fallon, Barack Obama, and Kim Kardashian, and then calculated their forward flow from sequences of tweets. Which brings us back to the Dalai Lama and Ariana Grande. The Dalai Lama is not *expected* to be divergent, overly creative, or provocative. We want our spiritual leaders to be consistent in their beliefs and time-held values and traditions. We want them to be inspiring, wise, humble. And when we see the low forward flow scores of the Dalai Lama, they reflect this type of thinking.

Ariana Grande, on the other hand, is recognized for her unconventionally strong and distinctive vocal range and as a charismatic, imaginative, inventive artist with a significant impact on music and pop culture. And her forward flow scores show this well.

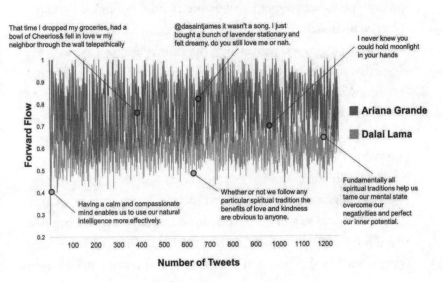

Forward Flow Scores of Representative Tweets from Ariana Grande and the Dalai Lama

Look Outside and See Yourself, Look Inside and Find Yourself

Forward flow highlights that we can accumulate all of our priors into a quantifiable measure of how predisposed we are to divergent thinking. This is a springboard to engaging in a more nuanced cultivation of something that impacts our gut feel. Step one, therefore, is *acknowledgment*. Acknowledging that we are relatively higher (like

Ariana Grande) or lower (like the Dalai Lama) in terms of divergent thinking.

Having an awareness of our own propensity for semantically distanced thought is one baseline trait. It is just one example, one category of self-understanding. There are many others that we can measure to understand our natural inclinations. For example, the Myers-Briggs Type Indicator categorizes individuals into one of sixteen personality types based on preferences in four dichotomies: extraversion vs. introversion, sensing vs. intuiting, thinking vs. feeling, and judging vs. perceiving. The Enneagram is a system that classifies individuals based on their motivations, fears, desires, and coping strategies. The Big Five model assesses openness, conscientiousness, extraversion, agreeableness, and neuroticism (or emotional stability), each considered to be a fundamental dimension of personality. These are some of the most popular tools. I encourage you to explore further.

You might want to understand specifics about your propensity for concentration and deep work, for example. The Concentration grid test is a simple assessment of attention and focus. You're given a grid such as this one. You start a timer and try to mark off each square in sequential order from 00 to 99. When you have crossed out every number, you are finished. Record your score. Then practice over the next few months, perhaps using the Pomodoro technique: Do all your work in short, focused bursts (typically twenty-five minutes) separated by a brief break (five minutes). This technique trains you to concentrate solely on the task at hand for those twenty-five minutes, knowing that you'll get a brief rest to recharge before the next interval. Retake the Concentration grid test periodically and record your time to mark your improvement as you strengthen your skills of concentration.

Concentration Grid

45	18	67	05	55	07	01	88	03	31
59	80	57	50	92	30	96	87	15	95
53	13	43	17	90	35	33	98	64	24
83	62	51	74	21	11	82	10	04	65
47	97	89	58	56	41	32	49	16	79
38	78	46	00	20	48	71	84	44	25
52	34	73	66	61	81	19	39	86	27
54	94	70	76	23	26	42	72	69	02
85	08	36	22	68	60	37	14	75	93
99	63	09	06	28	40	91	12	29	77

Another assessment you could do is one that measures cognitive flexibility, which refers to the ability to adapt your thinking and behavior in response to changing circumstances or demands. In essence, how good you are with change.

Or you might quantify your tendency toward hopefulness and optimism about the future by using the Hope Scale. Based on your score, you could then try to cultivate your own feelings of agency and belief in your ability to achieve goals.

The Resilience Scale is yet another tool that measures your ability to bounce back from adversity and overcome challenges. Cultivating and maintaining skills like adaptability, coping, and social support would be beneficial.

Two that have become favorites for many of the individuals whom I work with in my practice are the Procrastination Assessment Scale for Students, which measures individuals' tendencies to procrastinate, assessing various aspects of procrastination, including delay behaviors, reasons for procrastination, and consequences on performance, and the Impostor Phenomenon Scale, which assesses feelings of inadequacy, self-doubt, and fear of being exposed as a fraud despite evidence of success and competence.

All these assessments offer us valuable insights into specific aspects of our personality, behavior, and psychological functioning, helping us gain a deeper understanding of ourselves and our unique strengths and challenges. This information about ourselves will later help us activate our gut feel—whether we're aware of it or not.

Cultivation and Maintenance

Step two is *cultivation*. Returning to the concept of forward flow, once we understand our baseline, we can begin to ask ourselves questions that will help us cultivate, develop, and refine that baseline—so that we are better prepared when our intuition taps into a specific need for divergent (or convergent) thinking. Are the complex or chaotic problems that we are most often tasked with solving more like those that Ariana Grande must solve or those that the Dalai Lama is solving? If we are predisposed to convergent thinking (like the Dalai Lama), but we are often trying to solve problems that require more divergent thinking (like Ariana Grande), it's time to practice, develop, and broaden our propensity for divergent thinking.

We might research ways to practice thinking in a stream of consciousness, for example. While I was helping one of my clients with this, I discovered that James Altucher writes ten ideas a day to exercise his "idea muscle." He makes all kinds of lists, from business ideas to ways to surprise his spouse in bed to book titles that he thinks would be fun combinations of other book titles. We might practice divergent thinking by doing something similar, remembering that it's not about coming up with good or bad ideas—but about developing the practice of generating ideas, solutions, or possibilities and avoiding self-censorship during the process.

Step three, the final step, is *maintenance*. We might spend a day each month, reminding ourselves how everything connects—people, ideas, objects—and of our natural inclination toward divergent or convergent thought. Or we might notice when things connect and share that observation with a friend or loved one. One of my favorite quotes by Jim Jarmusch is this one: "Steal from anywhere that resonates with inspiration or fuels your imagination. Devour old films, new films, music, books, paintings, photographs, poems, dreams, random conversations, architecture, bridges, street signs, trees, clouds, bodies of water, light, and shadows. Select only things to steal from that speak directly to your soul. If you do this, your work (and theft) will be authentic. Authenticity is invaluable; originality is non-existent. And don't bother concealing your thievery—celebrate it if you feel like it, in any case, always remember what Jean-Luc Godard said: 'It's not where you take things from—it's where you take them to.'"

Tapping In

Acknowledging, cultivating, and maintaining—when you do this, great things can happen during the intuiting process. This is what happened for Paul Lancisi, without whom Pete Alonso may never have had his home run successes.

In 2019, Pete Alonso knocked out twenty-three home runs to win over Vladimir Guerrero Jr. in the finals of the Major League Baseball Home Run Derby. He beat a number of other heavy hitters, including Carlos Santana and Ronald Acuna Jr., and took home the winner's prize of $1 million. He won using a Dove Tail Bat, a baseball bat produced by a cabinet maker from the small town of Shirley Mills, Maine.

It has been said that started with a gut feel—but in actuality, it started with a commitment to be more creative and to engage in more divergent thinking. In the early 2000s, cabinetmaker Paul Lancisi was struggling with his business. Despite having built up a reputation for solid, functional cabinetry that lasted, he was getting outbid and outsold by competitors who had more creative designs. Knowing customers' preferences, he decided to focus on this weakness of his and try to understand why he was so hesitant to experiment—preferring function and purpose instead.

He thought about his working-class background and the emphasis that was always placed on avoiding waste because of the cost of materials. This introspection made him want to learn about the different materials he worked with: wood (such as oak, maple, cherry, or pine), engineered wood (such as plywood or particleboard), metal (such as stainless steel), and laminate. He found that each has its own aesthetic appeal, durability, and maintenance requirements. He played with the construction of his cabinets, using materials of different thicknesses and varied types of joinery (such as dovetail, dado, or mortise and tenon). He experimented with numerous styles, including traditional, modern, transitional, rustic, and contemporary. He made a practice of engaging in further introspection, connecting his own experiences with the properties of the material, sometimes forcing himself to stare at a piece of wood to visualize how it lent itself best to his personality and what he would want out of a custom design.

His cabinet business began to pick up, and by 2007, he was thriving. That same year, Lancisi was in his workshop one day when he spotted a bit of hardwood left over from a recently completed cabinet. It was just a leftover scrap, but he found himself staring at it, trying to "see" something. He noticed that the wood was great for dovetail joinery. And then he observed that the wood was almost in the shape of a baseball bat. His son, an avid baseball player, had been struggling with his swing recently.

Lancisi initially resisted and didn't allow his mind to go any further. "I manufacture cabinets, not baseball bats." At that point, his material was hardwood from Maine—northern white ash, yellow birch, and rock maple. *Perfect for baseball bats that would last longer and perform better because of how they could be shaped in such a way to have a "sweet spot," craft the vibration of the bat to take energy from the ball*, he thought. He allowed himself to continue thinking divergently. Resistance turned into openness. Lancisi experienced a sudden and unexpected shift in how he viewed the situation—a focused abstraction, if you will. Embracing a completely new angle allowed him to see the potential—and the need.

With that leftover hardwood, he crafted a baseball bat for his son. Not long after, Dove Tail Bats was formed and Lancisi began selling bats to men's leagues and tournaments nationwide. He manufactures custom wood baseball bats and now provides bats to amateurs and professionals throughout the US, Canada, Latin America, Australia, and Japan. In 2022 alone, Lancisi produced over thirty thousand baseball bats. Three of his bats have been inducted into baseball's Hall of Fame in Cooperstown, New York—including the one that Pete Alonso used to win the Home Run Derby, a bat that was made out of a leftover cabinet.

Practiced introspection had allowed him to tap into the muscles he later needed to reach this state of focused abstraction.

Mastering Your Intuition

Exercise: Understand the traits and characteristics that you personify. How do you describe yourself?

Take some time to think of your own traits and characteristics, acknowledging your strengths, weaknesses, and the ones you find most salient. Conduct tests and investigations, such as the forward flow test, to learn more about each one you'd like to acknowledge, cultivate, and maintain. Map them in terms of what stage you're in, not the extent to which you are strong or weak. For example:

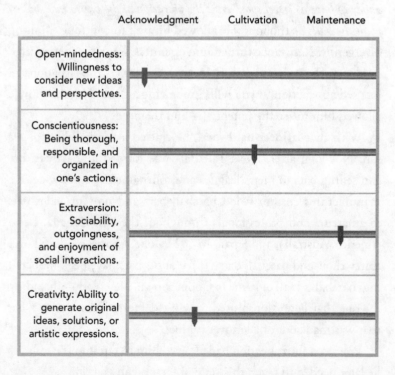

Use the following list as inspiration. Feel free to include as many or as few as you'd like or others beyond these. This list represents just a fraction of the many traits that individuals may possess. Each person is unique, and the combination of characteristics they exhibit contributes to their personality, behavior, and overall identity.

Open-mindedness:

Willingness to consider new ideas and perspectives.

Conscientiousness:

Being thorough, responsible, and organized in one's actions.

Extraversion:

Sociability, outgoingness, and enjoyment of social interaction.

Introversion:

Preference for solitude, quiet, and introspection.

Agreeableness:

Kindness, empathy, and cooperation toward others.

Neuroticism:

Tendency to experience negative emotions such as anxiety, worry, or moodiness.

Optimism:

Positive outlook, hopefulness, and expectation of favorable outcomes.

Resilience:

Ability to bounce back from adversity, setbacks, or challenges.

Creativity:

Ability to generate original ideas, solutions, or artistic
expressions.

Adaptability:

Flexibility and ability to adjust to changing circumstances.

Assertiveness:

Ability to express one's needs, opinions, and boundaries
confidently.

Perseverance:

Persistence, determination, and commitment to achieving
goals.

Empathy:

Understanding and sharing the feelings and perspectives of
others.

Self-discipline:

Ability to control one's impulses, emotions, and behaviors.

Leadership:

Ability to inspire, motivate, and guide others toward a
common goal.

Creativity:

Ability to think outside the box, innovate, and generate novel ideas.

Curiosity:

Eagerness to explore, learn, and seek out new experiences or knowledge.

8

Embodied: Where
Do I Feel That?

*Our embodied gut feel is honed when we perceive
where in our bodies we physically feel signals.*

My childhood friend Erin Earley is the creator of the Truth Test, which she (and many other therapists) use in their practices. It begins with grounding: Her clients go through a series of exercises to focus on their physical body and their breathing. They work on planting their feet and tuning into the sensations in different parts of their body.

After grounding, which is usually quite short in duration, they move on to baselining. Erin has them say their name. Say: "My name is *Gavin*." Again, say: "My name is *Gavin*."

She tells them to pause for a while and then asks them, "Where did you feel that?"

This determines where in their body they feel their truth. She finds that most people feel it in their chest (or in their upper gut). Sometimes Erin will ask them to state other obvious truths: their age, the names of their children, and so on. She tells me, "Almost everyone feels their truth in the same place, but people feel their lies in all different places."

She continues to prompt them, asking, "Can you feel your chest?" "Can you feel your stomach?" "Can you feel the sides of your arms?" And so on.

Once they know where they feel their truth, she has every single client, no matter who they are or where they come from, say the following line: "My name is Princess Phee Phee Phil."* And then she asks, "Where did you feel that?"

Sometimes it's in their stomach. Sometimes it's below their stomach. Many times it's in their neck and shoulders.

She continues to do baselining if she deems it necessary—having her clients state obvious truths and obvious lies: "I'm fifteen years old," if they're much older. "I'm seventy years old," if they're much younger.

Doing this helps her clients *reestablish* trust within themselves. For example, people who have been gaslit for years no longer know who or what to trust. They don't trust themselves because they've been told for so long that they're wrong, that what they feel, what their gut tells them is incorrect. The same goes for people who have been abused, physically or emotionally—they no longer trust their internal compass.

Finally, it's the truth and discovery stage. This is when Erin moves to harder questions. For example, she has her clients say: "I blame myself." She asks them where they feel that statement. And "If that's a truth for you, what does that mean to you?"

Erin talks about progress: when her clients no longer feel statements like that in their "truth locations" and how significant that is

---

* She tells me that people always giggle at first, but she makes them say it anyway. The same exact line.

for them. Or when they say, "I am not to blame," and they *feel* that in their truth locations.

She continues with gently probing questions like: "Can you tell me more?" and "And then what happened?" Ultimately, this starts to uncover what her clients (emotionally or logically) know (but don't trust themselves to know) because of trauma, negative experiences, or just getting stuck in their ways.* Importantly, it helps them recognize their own "notifications" so that they learn to recognize their triggers and internal "alerts" and tune their internal compass.

What Your Body Is Telling You

Warren Bennis felt it in his fingertips.

When Bennis became the twenty-second president of the University of Cincinnati, serving from 1971 to 1977, he said that he "wanted to lead with the passion and skills of a change agent and create a University of Cincinnati that would reflect all the social sciences that had taught us about human dynamics since World War II." In his role as president, he thrived and performed all his duties seamlessly. He attended endless social gatherings, gave speeches, and participated in forums and conferences. He answered questions about the university with panache, settling disagreements and reassuring audiences with his diplomacy.

During one particular forum, however, he fielded a question that caught him off guard. He was asked, "Do you like being a university

---

* There is an important fourth stage to Erin's Truth Test, where she "re-grounds" her clients to bring them "back" or bring them out of the exercise. She has them focus again on their physical body and their breathing to make the important transition "back" to one that is not quite so poignant and personal again.

president?" A long silence ensued. You could hear a pin drop. The silence hung in the air uncomfortably. Bennis felt a tingling in his fingertips, and then, finally, he answered, "I like the *idea* of being a university president." Shortly after that forum, he resigned from his post and went back to teaching, ignoring all the commentary about how he had "tumbled from his pedestal" and, even more harshly, "died from self-inflicted gunshot wounds." In 2014, at the age of eighty-nine, he said on his deathbed that his gut feel saved him from a lifetime of regret.

Today, Bennis is lauded for his research and teaching as a professor. He is still considered one of the world's leading experts on leadership, and a pioneer in his own right, serving as an advisor to four US presidents, including John F. Kennedy and Ronald Reagan.

During that post-question pause when the audience could hear a pin drop, Bennis felt the slightest tickling feeling in his fingertips. It was a personal signal that he had noticed before, the same sensation he experienced whenever new ideas came to him as he was researching and writing. It was his internal, embodied signal.

When I think of Warren Bennis, I can't help but be reminded of Philip Stone, who is a counterpoint to Bennis.

A pioneer in the field of positive psychology, Philip Stone was a professor of psychology at Harvard from 1960 until his death in 2006. In his obituary, he was referred to as a "timeless Renaissance man" who spent his entire career inspiring Harvard undergraduates. That's *almost* true. He did spend his career at Harvard. Except for one year. That was the year he took a sabbatical, and spent it teaching at Lewis and Clark College, a small liberal arts college in Portland, Oregon. He had a wonderful time there. He felt alive, invigorated, and had an excitement for his work like he had never experienced before.

In the decades that followed at Harvard, he would talk about his time at Lewis and Clark—but only to a select few, as most of the people in his network saw Lewis and Clark as a small no-name college. These colleagues couldn't even believe that he would have wasted *one* year of his life—his precious sabbatical year, no less—at such an unremarkable institution.

To an even smaller circle of comrades, Stone would allow himself to admit that that year at Lewis and Clark had been the best of his life and that, at the end of the year, the college had asked him to stay and join their faculty permanently. He had wanted to. But he was a Harvard professor. He reminded himself that not only was he a Harvard professor, he was a *tenured* Harvard professor. What would people think? What would people say?* Harvard, the crème de la crème. Status, power, prestige. There was no way he could actually stay at Lewis and Clark. He talked himself out of the desire to stay. He promptly returned to Harvard, never again leaving or daring to take another sabbatical.

On his deathbed, he revealed to one of his most trusted protégés that one of his biggest regrets was that he did not stay at Lewis and Clark, that he went back to Harvard. I can't help but wonder what would have become of Stone if he had stayed.

The Body Is Your Home

Everyone's embodied gut feel will be different. For years, I did not believe that I could find a spot where I "felt my truths," like Erin suggested was the case. But after more study of theories of embodiment in psychology and neuroscience, which suggest that

---

* What will people think? What will people say? These two sentences are responsible for more failed dreams than anything else in the world.

processes such as perception, memory, and language are closely linked to the body and its interactions with the environment, I realized that mine is a spot between my neck and left shoulder. It's normally always sore, and I find myself rubbing and massaging that area often. When I overeat, it physically hurts. When I'm uncomfortable, I notice an ache in that spot.

The reason we experience our gut feel physically in our bodies is because our actions and perceptions are intertwined, and our mind actually simulates sensory and motor experiences to understand and represent concepts and ideas. There are images and experiences that we've had that are grounded in bodily sensations. For example, perhaps I've spent much of my life writing and grappling with ideas, and that struggle is now associated with a stiffness that goes all the way from my writing hand, through my arm, elbow, and shoulder, to that specific point in my neck. Or perhaps I subconsciously recall that time I was at cheerleading practice, and was injured doing a stunt that left me bruised in that area—so each time afterward, I felt some anxiety doing that same stunt. I don't really know. But the process is situated in a specific context in which an interaction between the body, mind, and environment occurs. As George Lakoff and Mark Johnson found, we understand and express abstract concepts through metaphorical mappings grounded in bodily experiences. As early as the 1800s, psychologists and philosophers such as William James and John Dewey emphasized the importance of bodily sensations and emotions in shaping perception, thought, and behavior. For example, in social interactions, the concept of warmth is used to describe someone's friendliness, kindness, or approachability. According to James and Dewey, warmth is grounded in our bodily experiences of physical warmth and the associated sensations and emotions. Many would describe meeting someone new at a social gathering, and being greeted with a warm smile and a friendly handshake. Alongside that positive gut feel you have about that person, as you continue interacting with them, you may physically feel a sense of warmth through your body, and notice that you have a relaxed posture and are using open gestures. Your body hears everything your mind says.

Mastering Your Intuition

Exercise: Understand the areas of your body where you might be receiving signals. Identify where you feel things that your mind says.

Embodied Gut Feel Body Map

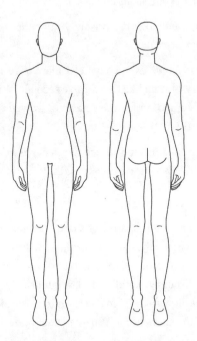

Mark each of the areas where you experience embodied gut feel.

If you don't immediately know or already have a sense, you might try a body awareness technique, which allows you to direct your focus to sensations that you have in your body.

- Place both feet flat on the floor. Wiggle your toes. Curl and uncurl your toes several times. Spend a moment noticing the sensations in your feet.

- Stomp your feet several times. Pay attention to the sensations in your feet and legs as you make contact with the ground.

- Clench your hands into fists, and then release the tension. Pay attention to the feeling of tension in your hands.

- Press your palms together. Press them harder and hold this pose for fifteen seconds. Pay attention to the feeling of tension in your hands and arms.

- Rub your palms together briskly. Notice the sound and feeling of warmth.

- Raise your hands over your head like you're reaching for the sky. Stretch like this for five seconds. Bring your arms down and notice the relaxation of your arms at your sides.

- Take deep breaths, and notice any feelings of calm in your body. Where are these areas? Indicate them on the body map.

As you become more aware of these areas of your body, notice where you physically feel comforting thoughts and uncomfortable sensations. For example, reflect on a painful situation that you haven't allowed yourself to fully think about or process the underlying emotions. Sit with the pain and the hurt. Instead of burying it, allow yourself to experience it. Where in your body do you feel it?

The first time you do this, you might have acute pain that feels like a tsunami; you might experience a tightness in your chest that feels like you're never going to breathe again (but you will).

Let some time pass (hours, or even days or weeks), and then try this a second time. It may still feel like a huge wave that is overpowering, even though it's less shocking and acute this time. Recognize where you feel it again in your chest.

Experience it a third time. Perhaps this time it will feel like a smaller wave. You may recognize that sensation in your chest once again. And then a fourth time, when it feels like a small ripple, and you start to recognize that not only can you get through that painful situation, you know where your area of embodiment is to help you do so.

Everyone is different. Some may feel a sensation of diminishing intensity in the same place. Others may experience it in an entirely different location in the body each time. Note what these differences are for *you*.

9

Emotional: How Do I Feel?

Our emotional gut feel is honed when we
understand our emotions and how they relate
to one another. This begins with tuning in,
so we can better identify them.

When we start to recognize *where* we feel things, we will naturally start to wonder *how* we feel things.

This is the emotional circumplex. It's a framework that can be used to organize and understand the emotions that we feel. James A. Russell, one of the most prominent researchers associated with the circumplex model of affect, showed how emotions could be mapped or categorized on a two-dimensional plane. Albert Mehrabian further contributed to the circumplex model with his work on pleasure, arousal, and dominance, showing how emotions and emotional responses could be influenced by various stimuli.

We can develop our intuition and our ability to experience a gut feel by mapping our emotions on this circumplex and having a baseline understanding of what emotions we typically feel and under what circumstances we feel certain emotions but not others—so that we are more attuned to those situations when we're feeling an emotion that's uncharacteristic or unexpected. As Gretchen Rubin says, "Emotions have an important role to play in life; they're big, flashing signs that you're on the right track or that something needs to change."

The Emotional Circumplex

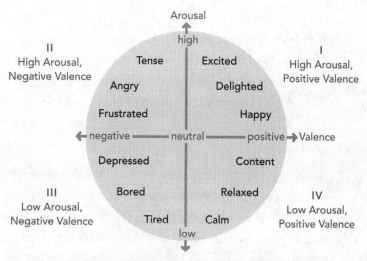

Liu, Zhe, Anbang Xu, Yufan Guo, Jalal Mahmud, Haibin Liu, and Rama Akkiraju. "Seemo: A Computational Approach to See Emotions" (2018): 1–12, 10.1145/3173574.3173938.

There are two dimensions that we can measure our emotions along: valence and arousal. Valence, the horizontal axis, refers to the pleasantness or unpleasantness of an emotional experience. David Watson and Auke Tellegen's work showed that there is positive and negative affect, with emotions organized around axes of positive and negative feelings, encompassing a broad range of experiences and dispositions that can vary in intensity, duration, and complexity. Emotions with positive valence are those that are typically experienced as pleasant, such as happiness, joy, and contentment. Emotions with negative valence are those that are typically experienced as unpleasant, such as sadness, anger, and fear. Valence represents the direction of an emotion along a continuum from positive to negative, with neutral emotions falling in the middle of the continuum.

Arousal, the vertical axis, refers to the level of physiological activation or intensity associated with an emotional experience. Emotions with high arousal are those that involve heightened physiological activity and are experienced as intense or stimulating, such as excitement, anxiety, and anger. Emotions with low arousal, on the other hand, are those that involve lower levels of physiological activation and are experienced as calm or relaxed, such as contentment or boredom. Arousal represents the intensity or energy level of an emotion along a continuum from low to high.

The emotional circumplex organizes emotions based on their position within these two dimensions, resulting in four quadrants. Emotions are plotted along this "emotional landscape" based on their valence and arousal levels, with similar emotions grouped together in close proximity.

Emotions Grouped by Valence and Arousal

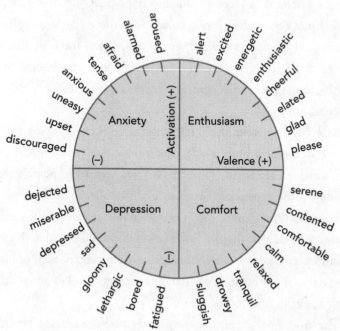

Ranta, S., H. Harju-Luukkainen, S. Kahila, and E. Korkeaniemi, "At worst it leads to madness." A phenomenographic approach on how early childhood education professionals experience emotions in teamwork, Nordisk barnehageforskning 19, no. 3 (2022).

We can map our emotions onto this emotional circumplex so that we understand the relationships between different emotions that we might feel. It provides us with a useful tool for understanding our own experiences, understanding how our emotions are related to one another, and even predicting our emotional responses in different contexts.

There's a picture that I once saw that continues to stay with me. It's of a little girl who's around two or three years old. She's sitting on the ground, she has a wound on her nose, and she has dirt on her face and clothes. She looks like she lives in the developing world, in horrifically unfavorable conditions. And yet she's offering some food to someone we can't see, who's outside the frame.

This picture tugged at my heartstrings and made me think. It's unforgettable. I couldn't identify exactly what emotions I was feeling at first, but when I was finally able to pinpoint them, I realized that I was first sad (Quadrant III) and then happy (Quadrant I).

A friend of mine, who is much less weepy and maudlin than I am, was immediately skeptical (Quadrant II), noting that the little girl looks healthy despite the conditions. Then she became angry (more of Quadrant II) at the photographer for taking advantage of the situation for their own gain or for virtue signaling.

When I showed the picture to other individuals, I saw that some had emotions squarely in one quadrant—they felt hope for the goodness of humanity (Quadrant IV), or they were like my friend who saw that this child was being taken advantage of for personal gain (Quadrant II)—or they were like me, shifting from one quadrant to another.

Emotions are a signal that we can recognize. But more than just noticing that we might be experiencing a particular emotion, if we understand our base emotions, our tendency toward a certain quadrant of emotions (especially when prompted by a particular type of problem or context) or our likelihood of shifting between quadrants, we will be better able to notice when how we feel doesn't conform to our usual patterns.

Emotional Indicators

There was a young biotech researcher named Saurabh who had been working on a project for months. He was invited to share his ideas and theories at a prominent conference in Dubai and was scheduled for an afternoon session of the conference. He listened to the morning presentations, all given by researchers much more senior to himself, on topics that seemed much more quantitatively complicated than his. Saurabh knew he didn't have time to change his presentation, 90 percent of which were images of proteins and the changes in protein activity that he had discovered.* It made him feel like he'd be reading a picture book to the audience, in contrast to all the other researchers who had disseminated weighty knowledge from encyclopedic volumes.

As he began his presentation and explained his unconventional ideas, he was met with skeptical looks and a few raised eyebrows. He felt a quick pulse of vulnerability and embarrassment go through him. A senior researcher interrupted him abruptly to ask a probing question, and Saurabh felt his cheeks flush—but in a moment of recognition, he realized that his embarrassment (and the researcher's abrupt question) hinted at the potential significance of his work. Saurabh realized that his ideas had struck a chord with someone who understood their profound implications.

Over the following weeks, Saurabh continued to refine his research and gather data. That senior researcher? He became his mentor and championed his project, and as the results started coming in, it became clear that Saurabh was indeed onto something big.

Saurabh told me that a signal that he often used to overlook is embarrassment. Working in a scientific field focused on discovery,

---

* In actuality, proteomics, the study of protein activity within cells, tissues, and organisms, has been instrumental in examining many functions, such as the formation of structural fibers of muscle tissue, enzymatic digestion of food, or synthesis and replication of DNA— research that has been critical to the discovery of many biotechnology medicines.

he's often operating in a state of high arousal—emotions related to ambition or determination on the one hand and impatience or distress on the other when things go wrong. He also observes a lot of high arousal (Quadrants I and II) emotions around him: self-superiority from senior researchers and disgust, envy, and hostility when there are turf wars and research battles.

That embarrassment, that pulse of discomfort—Saurabh now recognizes it as *the* turning point, *the* indicator of his gut feel. It was so oddly unfamiliar (as were his ideas, he later told me), that it perfectly cued him to a meaningful breakthrough.

Gut feel isn't your emotions. Your emotions are a symptom of gut feel, and those symptoms can be misinterpreted.

We cannot actually hone our emotions. Restraining them, burying them, trying to change them, or pretending that they are not there causes them to fester and gnaw at us. But we can hone our ability to recognize them as a signal that is telling us something.

Mastering Your Intuition

Exercise: Understand how to accurately recognize and identify your emotions. Understand how you feel things.

Using Russell's Circumplex Model of Affect, create your own emotional circumplex map. Highlight the ones that you find yourself feeling often. Look for patterns. If this isn't something that comes easily, or you don't know where to start, here are some suggestions.

First, begin by recognizing the four basic emotions: happiness, sadness, fear, and anger. Which of these do you feel and when?

Russell's Circumplex Model of Affect

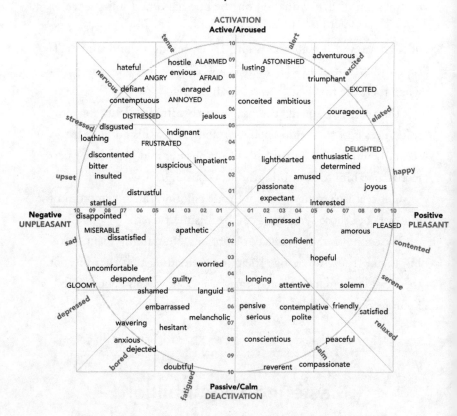

Posner, J., J. A. Russell, and B. S. Peterson, "The Circumplex Model of Affect: An Integrative Approach to Affective Neuroscience, Cognitive Development, and Psychopathology," *Development and Psychopathology* 17, no. 3 (2005): 715–734, https://doi.org/10.1017/S0954579405050340.

Start periodically labeling and noting down your emotions, thoughts, and experiences. This might be difficult at first. If you can't identify discrete emotions, just see where they fall in terms of the two axes of valence and arousal. From there, you can start to develop a vocabulary for your emotions, and practice identifying and labeling your feelings with specific words, such as *joy, anger, sadness,* or *anxiety.*

Write about different situations you face and identify whether you often operate from a single quadrant, or if there are certain patterns. As you do this, reflect on your emotional responses to various situations. Ask yourself why you feel a certain way and what might be contributing to those emotions. You'll start to notice "self-conscious emotions." While basic emotions such as anger, surprise, or fear tend to happen automatically, without much cognitive processing, the self-conscious emotions, including shame, guilt, and pride, are more complex. They require reflection and self-evaluation.

If you have trouble doing this, start by using anecdotes you've heard (but have nothing to do with you) or situations your friends are in. Try to put yourself in others' shoes and understand their emotions and perspectives. Contrast the emotions you feel versus the ones they might feel.

You can also try using example scenarios like the ones I include below. This will help you master your emotional gut feel.

Scenario 1: Sarah just received a promotion at work after years of dedicated service to her company. As she walked into the office that morning, her colleagues greeted her with applause and congratulations. Sarah's heart swelled as she realized that her hard work and perseverance had finally paid off. She celebrated the milestone with her team as they toasted to her success. The promotion not only brought Sarah personal fulfillment but also boosted morale and camaraderie within the team, creating a positive and uplifting atmosphere in the workplace.

Emotional quadrant: _____

Base emotions felt: _____

Shifting emotions: _____

Scenario 2: The CEO of a small start-up company faced a difficult decision to downsize the workforce due to financial challenges. Many of them had been with the company since its inception, pouring their hearts and souls into its success. The layoffs left a somber mood hanging over the office as colleagues hugged each other goodbye and cleared out their desks. Despite the necessity of the decision, the CEO couldn't help but be affected by the impact it had on the dedicated employees who had become like family.

Emotional quadrant: _____

Base emotions felt: _____

Shifting emotions: _____

Scenario 3: In the wake of a major data breach, the cybersecurity team at a large financial institution found themselves facing a daunting task. As news of the breach spread, panic rippled through the company, and the potential of further attacks loomed large. The cybersecurity team worked tirelessly to assess the extent of the breach, patch vulnerabilities, and implement new security measures to protect sensitive data. With each passing day, the pressure mounted as they raced against the clock to safeguard the company's assets and restore trust among customers and stakeholders.

Emotional quadrant: _____

Base emotions felt: _____

Shifting emotions: _____

Scenario 4: A manufacturing company discovered that one of its suppliers had been engaging in unethical labor practices, including child labor and unsafe working conditions. The CEO of the manufacturing company terminated the contract with the supplier and publicly denounced their behavior, vowing to uphold strict ethical standards throughout the company's supply chain.

Emotional quadrant: _____

Base emotions felt: _____

Shifting emotions: _____

Learning to identify your emotions is an ongoing process that takes time and practice. Be patient with yourself and embrace the journey of becoming more in tune with your emotions. You'll also notice the physical sensations that accompany your emotions and how different emotions manifest in your body, such as tension, butterflies in the stomach, or a racing heart. As you become more emotionally aware, you'll likely find it easier to navigate life's challenges, communicate effectively with others, and make decisions that align with your true feelings and values.

10

Cognitive: How Do I Construct Concepts?

Our cognitive gut feel is honed when we understand our schemas, mental models, and prototypes.

Read this description below. Read it as slowly or as carefully as you'd like.

A newspaper is better than a magazine. A seashore is a better place than the street. At first, it is better to run than to walk. You may have to try several times. It takes some skill but it's easy to learn. Even young children can enjoy it. Once successful, complications are minimal. Birds seldom get too close. Rain, however, soaks in very fast. Too many people doing the same thing can also cause problems. One needs lots of room. If there are no complications, it can be very peaceful. A rock will serve as an anchor. If things break loose from it, however, you will not get a second chance.

Take a piece of paper and draw these things: a house, a clock, a boy and a girl, and a ghost. Think about the description you just read. Jot down as much as you can recall from that passage.

On a scale of 1 to 10, how easy was it for you to remember details from the description?

Now let me add one piece of information about that passage for you: It's about flying a kite. Go back and read the passage again, and jot down what you can now recall.

On a scale of 1 to 10, how easy was it for you to remember things from that passage this time?

We'll come back to this in a bit. But first, go back to the clock you've drawn. Did you draw an analog clock?

More than 85 percent of people who do this exercise draw an analog clock. Yet most of the clocks that we see are digital, and believe it or not, one in six people can't tell time at all using an analog clock. So why are so many of us drawing an analog clock?

Look at the house you drew. Did the house look something like this?

Go back and put hands on the analog clock that you've drawn. Did you write the time as three o'clock?

What is going on? It's not sorcery. Kites, clocks, houses—they are all stored in our schemas, mental models, and prototypes, ready for retrieval. Our schemas, mental models, and prototypes inform our intuition and gut feel.

Organizing Is a Journey, Not a Destination

Schemas, mental models, and prototypes are three related but distinct concepts used in psychology and cognitive science to explain how individuals perceive and understand the world.

Schemas are generalized and allow us to quickly make sense of new information based on our existing knowledge and experiences. We can't store all the memories of all the clocks we've ever encountered so we have a simplified representation (a schema) of clocks in our mind. A schema is the reason we drew an analog clock and the house the way we did. Our schemas help us make generalizations so we can simplify our cognitive processing.

We do this even with more complicated concepts. Let's say you hear the word *restaurant*, for example. You are likely able to immediately and clearly envision the general concept of a restaurant. You might even think about specific features like a dining area, a kitchen, waitstaff, menus, and a variety of food options. This is your schema, and it might also include expectations about the typical dining experience, such as being seated upon arrival, ordering from a menu, and paying the bill at the end.

If I then said the word *house* to you, your mind would easily be able to switch to the concept of a house that you can elicit from somewhere in your memory. If I show you a photo of a house or take you into a house, even if you haven't seen it or been there before, you would still recognize it as a house. You recognize it because you have one or more schemas which have encoded the concept of what a house is. You have a general idea of what I mean when I say *restaurant* or *house*.

Mental models are more specific. Mental models are the reason it's easier to comprehend the passage about flying a kite once we know its subject.

When you're picturing your favorite restaurant, you know that that restaurant has swinging doors that lead to the kitchen. You know that there isn't a dessert menu because there's always a cake of the day, and you know that the bill will always come in a book, which is a gift for you.

At *your* house—the house you live in—you know that the bathroom is around the corner from the study, and that the shower tap needs to be turned in a particular way to make sure it doesn't leak. You know that one of the closet doors tends to stick, and that the best light comes from the windows in your bedroom.

All of this information based on your specific experiences and preferences is embedded in your mental model. And the experiences you've had flying a kite—the difficulties, the skill required, the age at which kite-flying was the most enjoyable—all of these factors provide information that help you cognitively process.

Schemas and mental models are cognitive frameworks used by individuals to make sense of the world. Schemas are broader cognitive structures that organize general knowledge and perceptions, whereas mental models are specific representations of how particular systems or phenomena work. Mental models can be seen as a subset of schemas, focusing on more specific aspects of understanding and prediction.

Prototypes are typified or idealized representations of what you believe are the most salient features or characteristics. A prototype is *the* mental model that you have deemed to be *the* way to do it. It's what you consider to be the best archetype—if you were to open a restaurant, it's the example that you would use to design *your* restaurant.

The mental model that you have of your favorite restaurant and the mental models that you have of all the restaurants that are familiar to you—these might all be *compared* with the prototype of your ideal restaurant. What you consider to be part of your prototype of a restaurant—you love swinging doors that lead to the kitchen, for example—might have impacted and influenced why you are drawn to your favorite restaurant (which also has a swinging door leading to the kitchen). When you are trying a new restaurant, you might be implicitly comparing it to this categorical prototype.

Schema: Restaurants in general
Mental model: Particular restaurants you have in mind and how they work
Prototype: An ideal restaurant

In this way, schemas, mental models, and prototypes can all vary from person to person, and are all influenced by cultural, social, and personal factors.*

This is important, because just as we all have different baseline traits and characteristics that we must be attuned to (personified gut feel), different parts of our body where we physically feel signals (embodied gut feel), and different emotions (emotional gut feel),

---

* These can also lead to biases or stereotypes. See my book *Edge: Turning Adversity into Advantage.*

Schemas	Mental Models	Prototypes
• A general framework or cognitive structure • Help us organize and interpret information about a concept or category • Help us filter and interpret information in our environment	• A cognitive representation of how something works or how elements of a system are related to each other • Constructed based on *your* individual experiences, knowledge, and understanding of a particular domain or concept	• A typical or idealized example of a category or concept that represents the most salient features or characteristics of that category • Help you categorize into your preferences

so, too, do we have different cognitive constructions of the world around us (cognitive gut feel).

For example, one person's schema related to a manager might be that managers are expected to have decision-making authority, while another person's schema might be that managers are expected to provide guidance and set goals, while allowing teams the discretion to make decisions where they have knowledge and experience. Likewise, each person's mental model of a manager will be a personalized cognitive representation of a specific type of manager—perhaps based on some combination of managers that they've had in their career thus far—down to their appearance and personality traits, how they're expected to communicate (e.g., whether they are approachable, strict, or supportive), and how they should handle different situations. And *your* prototype of a manager might be an idealized version of what your first boss should have been if they were a more effective manager. Your prototype might include qualities like strong leadership and good communication skills; or it might include qualities like fairness and the ability to motivate and inspire employees. It could encompass the idea that a boss is someone who is fair but firm, approachable, and open to feedback—or focus more on the expectation that a manager should have a clear vision for the team based on the organization's goals. It's a specific representation that is formed from your mental model.

The schema provides a general framework for understanding the role of a manager. The mental model is a personalized representation of a manager based on individual experiences and interactions. And the prototype represents that one idealized representation of the qualities and characteristics you've associated with an effective manager.

We can sharpen our cognitive constructs to help us navigate our interactions with managers, form expectations about their behavior and performance, and ultimately rely on our gut feel to make decisions—the way Oskar did.

Oskar, a student of mine, had a gut feel about Amir, the CEO of the start-up he had joined. The first time Oskar met Amir, his immediate thought was *He's either going to be rich or broke.* There was something unconventional about Amir that made Oskar want to reflect and understand more about where it was coming from. "I understood that Amir was someone big, with a big personality and big aspirations. He was going to be hugely successful and make audacious decisions. I just didn't *initially* know in what direction."

As Oskar and I explored this together, we were able to discern:

Oskar's schema: CEOs generally have big personalities.

Oskar's mental models: Particular CEOs like Elon Musk have faced financial difficulties in the past. In 2008, both Tesla and SpaceX were on the verge of bankruptcy, and Musk invested his own money to keep them afloat. Many CEOs have built vast wealth from humble beginnings, such as Jeff Bezos, who launched Amazon from his garage in 1994 as an online bookstore, and through strategic expansion and innovation, turned it into one of the largest and most valuable companies globally, making him one of the wealthiest individuals in the world. Oprah Winfrey, while not a traditional CEO, also built her media empire from humble beginnings. She started as a local news anchor, went on to host her talk show, *The Oprah Winfrey Show*, which became one of the highest-rated television programs, and created business ventures including Harpo Productions and the Oprah Winfrey Network, which contribute to her vast wealth.

As we continued talking, it became apparent that while Oskar had strong schemas and mental models about CEOs, he did not have a prototype.

So I sent Oskar on a mission to hone his cognitive gut feel. I suggested to Oskar that he reflect more on why he felt what was seemingly a Jolt by employing the Rule of 3, something that I use in my own interpersonal dealings. To apply the Rule of 3, I meet with someone three times, in three different situations, in order to get a "full enough" sense (at least according to my own heuristics) of who that person is.

Say I'm interviewing someone to be a new research assistant. I might have them come to my office first, a professional interview setting. Then I might take them to lunch for the second meeting so that I get to know them in a more casual setting. And finally, I arrange for them to come to a networking event, for example, which is a more social, group setting. It doesn't have to be over the course of multiple days or take a long time—sometimes it can happen back-to-back, or even within an hour or so. A formal interview, followed by a walk outside, capped off by a cup of coffee with a few other colleagues. It allows you not only to get a better sense of the person and see different signals that you might have missed if you're only observing them in a formal setting that they've prepared for, but it also allows you to get a better sense of *you*, and your priors, vis-à-vis them, and the new information and new perspective that they are bringing.

Oskar later shared with me how his Rule of 3 encounters unfolded with Amir. He discovered that initial Jolt, and the subsequent self-reflection that ensued, allowed him to realize something fundamental about himself and what his prototype of a CEO was. His schemas and mental models told him: It didn't matter if Amir was eventually going to be rich or broke—it was Amir's audaciousness that attracted him so fervidly. His prototype told him: The audaciousness, in essence, was the problem.

His prototype included benevolence, not audacity. It was a CEO with strong values—an idealized version of Yvon Chouinard, the founder and CEO of Patagonia from 2008 to 2020, who built Patagonia with a strong emphasis on environmental sustainability, corporate social responsibility, and ethical business practices, who even gave away the company in 2022 so the profits could be used to fight climate change. Oskar's prototype was on the other end of the spectrum from individuals like Kenneth Lay, the CEO of Enron Corporation, which collapsed in 2001 due to widespread accounting fraud and corporate misconduct, or Adam Neumann, co-founder of WeWork, who mismanaged his company with questionable financial practices.

Oskar realized, "I wanted to be someone big and successful, but not at the expense of my values. I had begun to take shortcuts and toe the gray zone in my life and had slowly, gradually, talked myself into thinking that it was okay or that anything I did that wasn't 'upper brow' would be just once."

Oskar left the start-up not too long after. He stayed in touch and remained friendly with Amir but kept his business dealings separate. Amir, in case you're wondering, is now being pursued in three different countries for fraud and embezzlement—after a glorious career for over a decade. He was both rich and broke.

Mastering Your Intuition

Exercise: Understand and identify your own schemas,
mental models, and prototypes. Understand
how you make cognitive constructions.

Use the Rule of 3 to build your awareness and your cognitive gut feel.

The basic idea behind the rule is that by cognitively processing three experiences with the same person, each time in a different context or with different parameters, you can gain more comprehensive insights into your schemas, mental models, and prototypes, and in turn, increase the likelihood of achieving a well-rounded understanding or solution through an awareness of your cognitive gut feel.

By involving other people, you tap into a variety of backgrounds, knowledge, expertise, and viewpoints. Each person will offer unique insights, opinions, and suggestions based on their experiences and perspectives. Conducting exploration or discussions at different periods allows you to capture how perspectives, circumstances, and opinions may evolve over time. What you think or feel about a topic at one moment may differ from your perspective at another. And finally, exploring something in different situations or contexts helps you assess how it may vary depending on the circumstances. Factors such as location, setting, environment, external influences, and other situational variables can all impact perceptions, attitudes, and outcomes, which allows you to uncover nuances, patterns, and considerations that may not be apparent when examining it in isolation or within a single context.

For example, as Thierry Marchand, who was once a French intelligence officer, told me, it's really easy to spot a charlatan* when you notice the pattern: They look like a caricature of what they are pretending to be. Every trait is too perfect and overly telegraphed. Real experts have unexpected traits and are imperfect. They are not trying hard to signal that they are what they say they are, so they give off many signals that you wouldn't expect.

Do this by simultaneously acknowledging that nothing is original. In today's society, unfortunately, we are obsessed with trying to *be* original, rather than making original choices based on our own gut feel. We all have overlapping schemas, mental models, and prototypes. What makes us truly original is the infinite number of topics that we have schemas, mental models, and prototypes of, the infinite number of combinations of experiences that we have that lead us from our schemas to our mental models to our particular prototypes, and the infinite number of directions and choices that we can make based on how our own schemas, mental models, and prototypes play out.

Pick a few contexts. Start with something simple, maybe movies. Note down any schemas, mental models, and prototypes you might have. Then try something more difficult and abstract like

---

* This is also true for "ambitious intermediates," who will do everything they can to mimic the caricature of an expert, believing it will get them there.

"light and shadows." And then take it up an even higher degree of difficulty and try it on something personal and vulnerable like your long-term "dreams and goals."

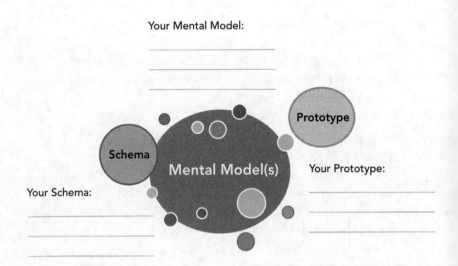

Your Mental Model:

Your Schema:

Your Prototype:

If you have trouble with this, return to the Rule of 3. Pressure test how you feel about your goals and passions, for example, with different people, at different times, in different situations. Note where you're more likely to be swayed by others, or where you're more skeptical of the opinions of others. Notice if there have been any recent events or news related to your thoughts on the topic that might be relevant. This allows you to see the best and worst cases, as well as any particular patterns that might exist. Importantly, it will allow us to tease out and consciously recognize ones that we might be implicitly defaulting to, which we will talk about in the chapters to come.

Interactions

11

What Does *Your* Eureka, Spidey Sense, or Jolt Feel Like?

It's where and how you feel it,
how you explain and organize it.

We can now take this understanding of our personified, embodied, emotional, and cognitive gut feel—to more deeply feel and recognize our *own* Eureka, Spidey Sense, and Jolts.

Let's start with Spidey Sense rather than Eureka, as we usually recognize our Spidey Sense most easily. Feelings of dissonance seem to present more noticeably. But even with Spidey Sense, remember that everyone's will be slightly different.

As I've mentioned, for me, there's this spot between my neck and my left shoulder that's always kind of sore, but I don't really notice it unless I'm really tired or when I overate. Sometimes when I'm caught off guard or field a question that I don't know how or don't really want to answer, I start to feel lightheaded and nervous. If you've read my book *Edge*, you know that when I get nervous, I giggle, even if I'm standing face-to-face with Elon Musk.

When I'm angry, it doesn't manifest as anger. I experience edginess or anxiety; it feels like I'm going to have to get into a verbal debate with someone, and I'm frustrated because it will likely be fruitless. (I get angry before calling customer service because I anticipate that they'll be incompetent at helping me, but I have no choice but to call customer service.)

I'm normally organized and particular to a fault. I'm structured in my thinking the way an engineer would be, even though I was a horrible engineer. I have almost no understanding of the animal kingdom, other than the fact that some animals seem scary or dangerous—it's a running joke in my family that I still don't know the definition of a mammal. I know that a duck-billed platypus is a mammal, though. When I'm caught off guard, I normally think less in terms of structures and more in terms of exceptions like this one.

I'm very attuned to the dynamics of social interactions and cultural norms and can navigate almost any social situation with empathy and understanding (except when I'm nervous). I'm comfortable with general financial and economic systems. For the life of me, I can't follow (or perhaps choose not to follow) politics, government, or law.

I see myself as an underdog, and I fail more than I succeed. I hate to fail, but I somehow also feel a surreal sense of peace during times of failure.

All of this coalesces into my own personified, embodied, emotional, and cognitive gut feel which resulted in a Spidey Sense I fortunately didn't ignore about one of my former colleagues,* an incredibly well-known, prolific Distinguished† Professor named Richard.‡

---

* And the very reason he is now a former colleague.
† Distinguished in his official title; not as an adjective.
‡ Not his real name.

When the Pieces Don't Fit

Richard and I were serving as committee members on a doctoral student's dissertation committee. In brief, a dissertation committee is a group of faculty members or professors who are responsible for guiding and evaluating a doctoral candidate's research and dissertation project. The committee is meant to play a crucial role in ensuring the quality, rigor, and academic integrity of the dissertation. Committee members provide feedback, advice, and assessment throughout the dissertation process, including proposal development, research execution, and the final dissertation defense—during which the candidate presents and defends their research findings before the committee to earn their doctoral degree. On this particular student's dissertation committee, there were four members, and Richard was the chair of the committee. The chair is usually the professor who is working most closely with the student, although status and seniority are also factors.

In March, about a week before this student was expected to defend her dissertation, Richard came into my office and started discussing Carla's research. This was not out of the ordinary. What was out of the ordinary was the nature of the conversation at this late juncture. Richard started alluding to his concerns about one of the chapters in her dissertation—a chapter that formed the basis of many of her claims and included hand-collected data. He believed the data to be invalid and needed to be eliminated from the dissertation. Richard went on to say that he had already spoken with the other committee members, each of whom had agreed with him, and that I was the last one he was reaching out to. He would be raising these issues at Carla's dissertation defense. The other committee members would be backing him up, and he was asking for my support.

The repercussions of this were serious. Although changes are often requested during the dissertation defense, they are often minor revisions—the type that would take a few weeks, or a month at most, to address. But an entire chapter, and an entire study with independent, hand-collected data? If this data were deemed invalid or even inadequate, Carla would not be permitted to include it in her dissertation, and in turn, she would have to take the time to re-collect and reanalyze data, and process and discuss all new findings—which could take many months, even years.

She had been anticipating a June graduation date, and had already landed an assistant professorship at an excellent research university. Based on what Richard was demanding, Carla would not only need to push back her graduation date to the following semester or the following year, but she would most likely have the professorship offer rescinded as a result.

I tried to process what Richard was saying. And *something didn't fit*. Two things immediately entered my mind. The first was a memory. Shortly after I joined the institution as an associate professor, Richard, who was already a full professor and senior in rank to me, sent me an email in which he wrote:

> I'm about to start working on a new project. Since I am refreshing on what is out there, can I request the names of the top folks whose works I might want to read and use to build on this project on the sociology of entrepreneurship. If you can give me the names of the top senior, mid-career, and junior (freshly minted) folks, and then do a review of their literature for me, I can then dig into their works.. i do

want variety and so hoping not to only cover work by senior folks.. [sic] I already have my own list in the making but was eager to see urs as I can then hopefully make sure I am not missing something.. [sic] A few pages lit review should suffice. Something that you'd except [sic] for a top journal.

I realized that he was asking *me* to do a critical piece of *his* research *for him*. My schema and mental model: A literature review is a survey of scholarly sources (such as books, journal articles, and theses) related to a specific topic or research question. It's written as part of a research paper, in order to situate your work in relation to existing knowledge, and it plays a key role in setting up the argumentation surrounding central hypotheses and interpretation of any pivotal findings discussed.

Richard was asking me to do something that he should be doing himself or, at the very least, by his own research assistants. It was very strange to be asking a colleague to do this, especially given an established researcher would presumably conduct a much more thorough and cohesive lit review. I found the way he was alluding to hierarchy and power dynamics odd, and the lack of respect that he was showing toward me, my own projects, and my own lit reviews offensive. It seemed like he was trying to get me to do his work . . . and then take credit for it.

The second thing that entered my mind was an awareness. Richard was working on his second book,* and he had included a few teasers in keynote speeches that he was giving to large corporations. In passing, Carla had once mentioned that she was working

---

* Or, as I suspect, a ghostwriter had completed the first draft and he had merely provided the "ideas."

on a slide deck of some of her findings so that Richard could help her get feedback from practitioners in the field, such as those working in the large corporations he was speaking to.

Something doesn't fit. I felt nervousness and anger, which I felt as anxiety and edginess. I felt a tightening in *that spot* between my left shoulder and neck, which accompanied a sense of dread over what I immediately recognized and understood to be true.

I don't know how I knew it, but I was sure that Richard's new book included Carla's ideas, data, and theories. Perhaps her work formed the entire basis of his book.[*] If so, Richard couldn't very well use this material for his book and claim it as his own if it was published first in Carla's dissertation. A pattern was forming in my mind, with constructs and causality, in a nomological network of interrelated variables.

So he was coming to my office and making up a bunch of reasons why she couldn't turn in that part of her dissertation so he could later stake a claim on it. And of course, as the chair of the dissertation committee and the sole chaired professor, who had the capability to derail my career as well as the career of each of the other committee members, he felt entitled to do so.

At that moment, with Richard staring down at me and expecting an answer, I played the good soldier and gave the impression of agreement to what he was asking. I knew in the back of my head that if I expressed my concerns or pushed back, that he'd find another way. He would get me kicked off the committee, replace me with another professor, or take a variety of other routes that I could hardly even fathom.

---

[*] Sadly, I later found this to be true.

After he left my office, I immediately went to one of the other committee members, an assistant professor named Boyce. As we talked, I realized that Boyce was also feeling extremely uncomfortable with Richard's request. I also realized that Boyce was not ready to put his own career on the line, as he said to me:

> Laura, you know how powerful Richard is. He is on the board of multiple Fortune 500 companies. He commands tens of thousands of dollars in speaking fees, just for showing up and giving a 30-minute keynote. He's a best-selling author. He knows tons of people. AND, he's going to be voting for our tenure cases in the big room. You know that one negative comment is all it takes. One black ball. Any concern that he raises, any inkling of doubt about our suitability for tenure—you know the impact it would have on our career. He is buddies with all of the associate deans and chaired professors in our field.

I didn't even need to talk to any of the other committee members, each of whom was even more junior to Boyce and me, to know that they shared the same sentiment. They couldn't afford to put their careers on the line. Neither could I.

But neither could I put Carla's career on the line and still be able to face myself in the mirror.

On the day of the defense, I did not out Richard. I knew that no one would believe me, and that no one would back me up.* But

---

* How did I know this? Because I had already experienced the underbelly of academia twice before, as I'll later share.

I did try to save Carla. In front of the entire audience, I preempted Richard and made sure to draw attention to the validity and suitability of the data—Carla's data: "I want to draw particular attention to how well chapter three of Carla's dissertation was done. I have had numerous conversations with her about her data, dating back to over a year ago. She hand-collected all of the data herself, coded all of the data herself, and I think we can all agree how well that work was done."

As I continued to talk about this particular data set, citing hard evidence about its validity, I could see Richard's face harden out of the corner of my eye. He was stuck. In the middle of a dissertation defense, with an audience of scholars and academics, he had no way to voir dire what I was saying in the heat of the moment.

The other committee members were deathly quiet. Boyce looked extremely uncomfortable, sick, even—he's a good guy at heart, and I knew he was scared for me and my career.*

Carla passed her defense.

Pinpointing Spidey Sense

Recall that we have a Spidey Sense when something feels off from what we know to be true. We receive a prompt (new information or new experiences) that doesn't align with our priors and results in a

---

* I left this institution shortly after, which I'll talk about more in the last chapter. Nearly everyone told me I was crazy to leave a university that millions would kill to be a part of. But I had learned a hard lesson. A good friend of mine who is still at the institution encapsulated it perfectly. He said, "There are two types of people at this school: those who throw other people under the bus to protect their own careers, and those who throw other people under the bus for game." Obviously, that schema and mental model of his was a bit tongue-in-cheek, as there are good people everywhere if you look hard enough. But you get the point.

feeling of dissonance or discord. "Something comes along that just feels wrong."

For me, this is what it looks like:

Personified: Structured, assertive, empathetic	**Embodied:** Sharpness in the spot between my neck and my left shoulder
Emotional: Anger in the form of anxiety (negative valence, with high-to-mid arousal)	**Cognitive:** Schemas of failure over success Mental models of underdogs Prototypes of Mulan, Andy Dufresne

I've described my own inputs, but it's my cognitive gut feel that takes primacy during my Spidey Sense moments. For many, it's their embodied gut feel; they might feel tightness in their chest, pain in their abdomen, or a sinking feeling in their stomachs. My emotional gut feel is secondary. I feel anger in the form of anxiety. Others may feel a similar sense of unease or nervousness, as if something isn't quite right, even if they can't articulate why.

This is not to say that my personified gut feel and embodied gut feel don't play a role. They do, but I know my telltale signals and how they present strongest through my cognitive and emotional gut feel.

Remember, everyone's manifestation of Spidey Sense, as well as Eureka and Jolt, will be different, so we must sharpen our understanding of our sensations.

Mastering Your Intuition

Exercise: Understand how your personified, embodied,
emotional, and cognitive gut feel come together
to produce your Spidey Sense moments.

Almost everyone describes their Spidey Sense as a "sensation of danger or uneasiness." Which of these scenarios makes you feel the most uneasiness or gives you a sense of discomfort, concern, or apprehension?

A. Social situations, meeting new people, attending social events where you don't know anyone, or being in large crowds

B. Being in conflict or tension with another person or within a group, including disagreements, arguments, or unresolved issues

C. Going through significant life changes or transitions, such as starting a new job, moving to a new place, or ending a relationship

D. Phobias that make you feel like you're in a dangerous or threatening situation

E. Being confronted with moral or ethical dilemmas, such as witnessing injustice, facing ethical conflicts at work, or feeling conflicted about personal values

F. Experiencing symptoms of illness, undergoing medical procedures, or facing uncertainty about your health or the health of a loved one

G. Being in environments that feel unsafe, uncomfortable, or overwhelming, such as crowded or poorly lit spaces

H. Feeling self-conscious about your appearance, abilities, or social status, or worrying about how others perceive you

Choosing the one that makes you feel the *most* uneasy, give yourself another few minutes to put yourself in a situation of that place, time, and context.

Now ask yourself these questions, and try to fill in your own mental map of what might be going on in terms of your inputs when you are feeling a Spidey Sense:

Personified: Which traits feel like they are under attack or at risk?	**Embodied:** Where do I feel physical discomfort?
Emotional: What emotions are contributing to my sense of agitation and sense of discomfort?	**Cognitive:** What topics come to mind when I feel a lack of clarity? What themes would come up, if I were trying to get alternate points of view on this from others?

Which quadrants were easiest to fill in? Which quadrant seems to take primacy? Which secondary?

Pinpointing Eureka

We can do the same for our Eureka moments, which should now be easier to pinpoint since we can compare and contrast it with our Spidey Sense. If you recall, Eureka moments are about generating insights, which is why it's often described as an *aha* or *light bulb* moment—a quick realization that often comes after a period of contemplation, problem-solving, or creative thinking.

It's the type of sensation you might feel when you grasp a solution, connection, or understanding that had previously eluded you:

> In the land of the Moors, you come across their most famous entryway, which they call the Green Glass Door. It's a powerful door, one that only lets certain people and certain belongings of these people through the door. Zookeepers are allowed through, but veterinarians and doctors are not. Ballerinas are allowed through, but gymnasts and musicians are not. Moose and deer can enter, but antelope and elk are denied. Pepper can be brought through, but not salt. You'll find that books have gone through, but only if they are not novels or encyclopedias or dictionaries. No magazines either.

This is one of my favorite riddles, and each time I share it with someone, I get to see that Eureka moment in real time. Don't let me spoil it for you—see if you can figure out the riddle yourself. See if you can name three items that are allowed entry and three reciprocal items that are not. Salt and pepper: Pepper can be brought through, but salt cannot. Ducks and geese: Geese can gain entry, but ducks cannot. Shoes and boots: Boots can walk through; shoes cannot.*

---

* When you're ready for the solution, or when you think you've got it: It's the Green Glass Door. *Green, glass, door.* Each of these has a double letter in its spelling. Any word that is spelled with a double letter can go through the green glass doors, but any word that isn't spelled with a double letter can't. Get why it's the land of the Moors? So grass can get through, but not flowers; a happy person, but not a sad person.

Here's how Adam, one of the world's top cardiac electrophysiology physicians in the world, described the sequence of events that led to one particular Eureka moment. Adam is originally from the UK, but he and his wife and two kids lived on the East Coast of the US, where they own a home. From time to time, his wife talked about moving back to the UK—it's home, after all, and many members of their extended family still lived there. Adam got a phone call from a work friend who told him that he was leaving for a great opportunity in the UK, and that the company was hiring for a second position that would be well suited for Adam. That same day, Adam received a phone call from his aging father who said, "I think you should live closer to us and find a job that is closer, even if you have to take a step down." It was an odd comment, as his father had always told him to "go to where the work is" and make sacrifices to provide for his family. At the time I was interviewing Adam, he was struggling with this dilemma: Should he relocate his family? He thought, *Maybe now is the time.* But he reminded himself of the house they owned, which they had tried to sell multiple times over the past few years, in an effort to downsize. They never got the price they wanted, so each year, they took it off the market and decided to keep living there. And what about his job? His wife and kids? What about the time, cost, and resources required to make such a big move?

He saw that his father valued time differently now that he was older. He remembered a quote from *The Alchemist*, one of his favorite books: "If you send things out into the universe, the universe gives you signals back." He wasn't sure if that was the actual quote, but he felt an embodied response, first. Adam recognized his significantly heightened senses, sometimes accompanied by a slight fluttering in his stomach, and thought: *Eureka!*

Adam describes feeling Eureka moments physically, seemingly more than others do (whereas he does not feel Spidey Sense moments physically as much as others do). His senses are acutely involved: His eyes widen and his hearing is amplified. There is also a large cognitive gut feel component, in that he has certain books that he's read at the edge of his consciousness—like how he thought about *The Alchemist* by Paulo Coelho, a story told from the perspective of Santiago, a young Andalusian shepherd who sets out on a journey that takes him from his home in Spain across the deserts of Africa. Santiago encounters a series of characters who guide him and offer wisdom, including a mysterious king, a crystal merchant, an Englishman seeking to uncover the secrets of alchemy, and an alchemist who helps him understand the deeper meanings of his quest, with each encounter teaching Santiago important life lessons about following his dreams, listening to his heart, and recognizing the interconnectedness of all things.

Adam and his wife discussed putting the house back on the market again, with no expectations. They would set their price—what they would need to recoup to make their move—and this time, they would not stage the house or do open houses. They would continue to live there without making any extraordinary efforts to sell their home. They received four offers, all above their asking price.

Then he sent his résumé and talked to the hiring manager about his qualifications.

Each signal he received, from each action he took, led him to the next interconnected action. And each was a sound one.

Moving costs would be high, taking the new job would result in a pay cut, and he had his children's education to consider. But as he accounted for all the variables and as he talked with his wife in earnest about the decision, he saw how he'd be saving money by not having to pay for private schools—and his parents would be around to help.

Here is how Adam described his Eureka moment:

Personified: Piqued curiosity, accomplishment	Embodied: Slight fluttering in his stomach, heightened senses
Emotional: Excitement, with a strong desire to tell and share with others (high arousal, positive valence)	Cognitive: Schemas of discovery and novelty Mental models of really unique books, with thought-provoking topics Prototypes: specific books such as *The Alchemist*

The telltale sign of a Eureka moment for most is a sensation of how new, yet surprisingly familiar something is. As Raymond Loewy, the French American industrial designer (who was responsible for the Coca-Cola fountain dispenser, the interior of the Concorde and the Apollo spacecrafts, streamlined locomotives for the Pennsylvania Railroad, and designed the logos for Exxon, Shell, BP, Nabisco, Quaker, and the US Postal Service), once said, "To sell something surprising, make it familiar; and to sell something familiar, make it surprising."

There is scientific support for why this happens. Guenther Knoblich and Michael Öllinger, who have studied how sudden, smart insights arise, say that the sensation itself can be attributed to the moment when the right hemisphere of the brain has sent a solution to the left hemisphere of the brain, thereby putting the solution into discernible terms. That link has been created between something familiar and something new. It's not revolutionarily new; it's not radically new; it's optimally new*—it contains a familiarity, which enables that light bulb moment when you are presented with something that would otherwise seem foreign.

More physiologically, Giulia Sprugnoli and colleagues have found that this seems to be related to stimulation of the right temporal lobe and the prefrontal cortex—which is in accordance with converging EEG and neuroimaging evidence—suggesting a clear neurophysiology underpinning to Eureka moments.

Adam, who now lives in the UK, told me recently that his decision to move helped him understand what it meant to have a "true north." *This* decision was about *heading* north, progressing ever upward, solving a problem with each step. For other decisions, it was about *discovering* north and discerning how the signals from the universe and his own gut feel seemed to be pointing in a specific direction.

---

* Harvard Business School professor Karim Lakhani popularized the term *optimal newness*; Loewy called his theory *MAYA* for *Most Advanced Yet Acceptable*.

Mastering Your Intuition

Exercise: Understand how your personified, embodied, emotional, and cognitive gut feel come together to produce your Eureka moments.

When you figure out a problem or have an aha moment, just like Adam did, take note of how you experience that clarity and certainty. Observe how you might feel a sense of surprised excitement or how the moment seems vivid and memorable. Recognize the urge you might have to share it with others.

Take a look at the scenarios below. Which of the following makes you feel most excited yet settled, with a sense of accomplishment over your discovery, realization, or insight? Choose one that feels deeply rewarding and satisfying.

A. Figuring out the solution to a challenging riddle or brainteaser that you've been struggling with for a while
B. Finding a creative work-around to a problem or a difficult situation
C. Having a burst of creative inspiration while working on a project (a paper, painting, or piece of music)
D. Suddenly grasping a difficult concept while studying for an exam or trying to learn a new skill
E. Seeing something cool and unexpected in the natural world, like an interesting plant or fascinating animal behavior
F. Having a moment of self-discovery or gaining a new perspective on your life, a belief, or a close relationship

Reflecting on that scenario, fill in your own mental map of your Eureka moment by answering the following questions:

Personified:	Embodied:
Which traits are responsible for my sense of clarity and understanding?	Where do I physically feel childlike openness and wonderment?
Emotional:	**Cognitive:**
What emotions do I feel when I have a rush of enthusiasm?	What topics evoke surprise and awe in me?

Pinpointing Jolts

Some describe their Jolts as "an abrupt realization or moment of recognition," which leads them to easily confuse it with Eureka moments. But remember, whereas Eureka confirms what you already knew, a Jolt changes your perspective on what you *thought* you knew—it changes your mind. Others say they experience it as *feeling the force* of a mysterious energy field à la Star Wars.*

Like a Spidey Sense, there is dissonance and discord. Something doesn't fit. But a Jolt is about realizing that something about your priors is wrong (or is no longer right for your circumstances and station in life). New information, or that new experience you had, has caused you to see that. Whereas a Spidey Sense is about holding firm to what you knew and believed before because the new infor-

---

* A force created by life that binds the galaxy together. Harnessing the power of the Force gives the Jedi, the Sith, and others sensitive to this spiritual energy extraordinary abilities, including telekinesis, mind control, and clairvoyance.

mation is trying to lead you off course, Jolt is about the new information trying to steer you in a different direction and you letting go of what you believed before. It's what Taruo Yabe experienced.

Taruo Yabe was the director and general manager of Tessei, a railway maintenance company responsible for cleaning the Shinkansen bullet trains, a network of high-speed railway lines in Japan. The Shinkansen trains are an engineering and operational marvel, running at 320 kilometers (or two hundred miles) per hour and always within fifteen seconds of schedule. Trains have a twelve-minute turnaround time, with five minutes allotted to getting current passengers off and new passengers on, and seven minutes for cleaning in between.

In those seven minutes, a twenty-two-person Tessei crew is tasked with cleaning one thousand seats, wiping down all the tray tables, replacing the seat and headrest covers, and rotating the seats 180 degrees so they face the new direction of travel. They must also clean the floors and bathrooms, empty all the wastebaskets, collect any forgotten items from under the seats or in the overhead bins, adjust the window blinds, and generally make sure everything on the train is neat and tidy. Workers at Tessei consider their jobs to be dirty, difficult, and dangerous—and Yabe was facing several challenges with his workforce, including a decrease in employee productivity, a lack of communication and trust between employees and management, and a growing divide between the older and younger employees.

In addition to grappling with these issues of low employee morale and public perception of cleaning as an undesirable job, he also needed to drastically reduce the cleaning time to maintain the tight schedules of the trains.

Yabe's Jolt came when he realized that he had been seeing his company as a *cleaning* company, when, in fact, it was a *hospitality* company.

<table>
<tr><td>

Personified:

Risk aversion, an initial sense of resistance, followed by openness

</td><td>

Embodied:

An intense, deep feeling of churning in his stomach

</td></tr>
<tr><td>

Emotional:

Disbelief and frustration, followed by pensiveness and solemnity (moving diagonally from high arousal, negative valence to low arousal, positive valence)

</td><td>

Cognitive:

Schemas of reflection and self-exploration

Mental models of meditative and breathing states

Prototype of the philosopher D. T. Suzuki and Zen philosophy

</td></tr>
</table>

For Yabe, his personified and emotional gut feel were the strongest signals. What was interesting was that for each of these, he experienced duality—both resistance and openness, as well as both frustration and calm pensiveness.

On the one hand, he understood that his workforce had an essential role in maintaining the Shinkansen's reputation for cleanliness and punctuality. On the other, to accomplish this, there needed to be a commitment to both passenger welfare and operational excellence. The link between the two: pride. A sense of purpose and pride in the Tessei employees, which would be accomplished by first changing the public perception of these workers, so that, in turn, it would foster a sense of pride among the cleaning staff.

He thought about his own schemas and reflected on how in Japan, the public looked down upon cleaners, although they valued and respected hospitality and superior service. After making the bold stroke to change Tessei's primary objective from cleaning to hospitality, he went to work on the long march. He changed employee uniforms to a bright red (so that rather than hiding in shame, these employees drew attention as the representatives of the brand); he instituted interactions with passengers (even providing stickers and toys that employees could give as small gifts to young children); he introduced angel reports to acknowledge "out-of-the-ordinary work" that might have otherwise gone unnoticed with monthly and annual cash awards; and he collected and *implemented* staff recommendations for improvement (for example, bowing to customers at the beginning and end of cleaning, cleaning all trays instead of just the dirty ones, and soliciting trash directly from customers).

This turned Tessei into a model of operational excellence and customer service, significantly reducing cleaning times while maintaining high standards. Yabe's efforts showcased the importance of valuing and empowering employees to achieve outstanding results. His physical, emotional, embodied, and cognitive gut feel manifested as a Jolt and shifted Yabe's mindset from cleaning to hospitality, resulting in Tessei's remarkable transformation.

Mastering Your Intuition

Exercise: Understand how your personified,
embodied, emotional, and cognitive gut feel
come together to produce your Jolts.

Like Yabe, you may have experienced a similar type of Jolt. Perhaps you listened to it, and made some type of change in your personal or professional life. Perhaps you didn't. When you feel that Jolt, when you have a realization that leads to a fundamental shift in your thinking, pay attention to any initial resistance that you might feel, which is followed by openness and candor. Note any feelings of disbelief that you might have early on, and how in turn, those heighten your senses in an intense and profound way. Observe your desire to explore and reflect on the shift that is occurring.

Consider the following scenarios. Which of these make you feel like you're redefining a part of yourself or your life?

A. Downsizing to a smaller home, upsizing to a larger home, or changing your housing and living arrangements
B. Ending a toxic friendship or forging a new, fulfilling friendship with someone you just met
C. Switching to a completely new diet; for example, a plant-based diet when you were a big meat eater
D. Transitioning from atheism to Christianity after a profound spiritual experience
E. Changing career paths
F. Embracing existentialism after grappling with questions of purpose and meaning
G. Trying a different fashion style; for example, embracing a minimalist look to promote simplicity

Now answer these questions:

Personified:

Which traits are in play when I feel like I am resisting and avoiding something?

Embodied:

Where do I physically feel profound, deep experiences?

Emotional:

What emotions do I feel when I am in a state of surprised disbelief?

Cognitive:

What topics evoke intensity and shifts in my behavior or thinking?

Nelson Mandela once said, "A simple jolt is all it takes to change the course of your life forever." The key is recognizing when there might be a paradigm in your life that is shifting so that you can decide what should change alongside it.

12

Focused Abstraction

*Life teaches you the wisdom that you can't get
from education alone. It's the wisdom that always
seems to come gradually, then suddenly.*

Ernest Hemingway's 1926 novel, *The Sun Also Rises*, is about a group of expatriates who try to navigate post–World War I disillusionment and aimlessness. Mike Campbell, one of the characters, is a wealthy man who finds himself in financial ruin due to his reckless spending and gambling habits.

"How did you go bankrupt?" Bill, an acquaintance who shares a common lifestyle in postwar Europe, asked.

"Two ways," Mike replied. "Gradually, then suddenly."

Hemingway encapsulates the essence of how significant changes often occur in life—things often build up over time, almost imperceptibly, until they reach a tipping point and manifest suddenly and dramatically. In Mike's case, his financial downfall is a slow and steady decline, marked by small losses and poor decisions, until he eventually reaches a point of crisis where everything falls apart.

But this also describes exactly how reaching a state of focused abstraction occurs: Our experiences, observations, data, priors, and prompts all build up gradually until they reach a critical threshold and then unfold suddenly and unexpectedly. It also underscores the importance of paying attention to subtle signs and taking proactive steps, even when we think we've reached the "endgame."

A Single Drop Creates Ripples

In 1996, John Osher thought he had reached that endgame when he accomplished the ultimate business objective that he had been striving to achieve. He had created a successful product and sold it. That product, the Spin Pop,* was a lollipop with a battery-operated handle that twirls candy in the eater's mouth after you push its signature Try Me button. In 1997, he sold Spin Pop to the toy division of Hasbro for $120 million, and the candy continues to be sold around the world today.

Not long after completing the Hasbro deal, Osher was in Walmart one day, when he noticed that all of the electric toothbrushes "were all packaged in fancy boxes, cost at least $80 each, and I couldn't try any of them." He was surprised by this, and then felt himself transported to a different plane of recognition. Osher had reached a state of focused abstraction.

His lollipop was not the endgame. Indeed, Osher now jokes that his toothbrush solved the problem that his lollipop created. His Spin Pop had employed small gears and was handheld and battery-operated. The lollipop had merely provided him with the experience and the road map for a greater creation: an inexpensive

---

* To be precise, the earliest Spin Pop was invented by four postal workers, after which Osher acquired the invention and developed it. Osher has said that he is always searching for interesting ideas or unfilled niches. "I live in a posture of looking. . . . I compare it to somebody who writes jokes. They see jokes where other people don't. They might look at that book over there and get inspired to write a joke."

electric toothbrush with a battery life of at least three months that cost only $1.49 to manufacture and retailed for $5. Osher and his partners had created the first low-cost, mass-marketed mechanical toothbrush—which was sold to Procter & Gamble* in 2001 for $475 million.

As you recall, focused abstraction refers to a mental state in which we're able to focus on a particular sliver of information that is part of a larger task, problem, or concept while simultaneously maintaining a broad perspective and being brought to a higher dimension or range of possibilities. In this state, we're able to filter out distractions and immerse ourselves fully in the task at hand, allowing for sustained attention to and deep engagement with the particular problem we're trying to solve.

The "abstraction" piece refers to the process of mentally distilling complex information or concepts into simplified and generalized representations. In the context of focused abstraction, this involves the ability to extract the essential elements or patterns from a complex situation and focus attention on them while disregarding irrelevant details.

This leads many to assume that a state of focused abstraction is achieved by concentrating deeply, eliminating distractions, and practicing mindfulness—deep breathing exercises, meditation, or visualization to help calm your mind and enhance your ability to focus.

In fact, the best way to hone your ability to reach a state of focused abstraction is to maintain flexibility in your thinking and approach, especially in the areas where you have the most expertise.

---

* Osher and his team aren't done. Keep an eye out for the Dish Doctor, a battery-powered dish scrubber.

Mastering Your Intuition

Exercise: Understand where you might be focused to the point
that you only notice suddenness—or where you might be
distracted to the point that you only notice gradualness.

Next time you are brushing your teeth, pay attention to the motions
that you are making. Notice the fine motor skills, coordination, or
precision that is involved. Think about the experience and the neural connections and habits in the brain that have been developed
over decades that have made toothbrushing an automatic activity
for you.

Then switch hands. If you're right-handed, use your left hand,
and vice versa. Again, observe your coordination, precision, and
experience. You'll inevitably make note of the initial difficulty, but
then you'll focus your attention on smaller details—like the place-
ment of a particular finger, stiffness and awkwardness in a specific
part of your wrist, or even tenderness in one of your teeth that you
didn't notice before.

By engaging in this very simple everyday activity with your
nondominant hand, you are promoting neuroplasticity and cognitive development. You are allowing yourself to notice "the gradual"
in a simple and accessible manner, while also reminding your brain
of its remarkable ability to adapt and grow and notice "the sudden"
that can come in response to new challenges and experiences. This
helps you hone your ability to get to and recognize when you've
arrived at a state of focused abstraction.

Continue to hone this by experimenting with other variations.
Switch the hand you use for other daily tasks, such as writing, eating, or using a computer mouse. If you're a musician, play with your
dominant hand and gauge your familiarity with the music and the
technique—and then try playing a simple chord or scale using your

nondominant hand. You could also try activities that are in completely different domains, like taking different routes to work than you're normally accustomed to, for example.

Again, what you're doing is enhancing your brain's ability to adapt in response to novel experiences. Your brain is forming new neural connections and pathways,* strengthening existing ones, and improving its ability to learn.

Once we harness neuroplasticity in simple, everyday tasks, we can apply it to more conceptual experiences. Travel and going on new adventures are ways to gain exposure to fresh perspectives that allow us to practice getting to a state of focused abstraction in a broader sense.

I love this quote by Henry Rollins:

> I beg young people to travel. If you don't have a passport, get one. Take a summer, get a backpack and go to Delhi, go to Saigon, go to Bangkok, go to Kenya. Have your mind blown, eat interesting food, dig some interesting people, have an adventure, be careful. Come back and you're going to see your country differently, you're going to see your president differently, no matter who it is. Music, culture, food, water. Your showers will become shorter. You're going to get a sense of what globalization looks like. It's not what Tom Friedman writes about, I'm sorry. You're going to see that global climate change is very real. And that for some people, their day consists of walking twelve miles for

---

* In essence, you are engaging multiple neuroplastic mechanisms, such as synaptic plasticity and cortical remapping, which lead to structural and functional changes.

four buckets of water. And so there are lessons that you can't get out of a book that are waiting for you at the other end of that flight. A lot of people—Americans and Europeans— come back and go, "Ooh," and the light bulb goes on.

Another way to encourage our brains to achieve a state of focused abstraction is by having lots of different types of conversations. Switch up your conversations like you would your dominant hand while playing guitar:

- Challenge yourself to initiate conversations on diverse topics. Start with familiar subjects, and then gradually explore new and unfamiliar topics, even ones that might scare you.

- Experiment with different communication styles and approaches, such as being more assertive in some conversations and more empathetic or supportive in others. Practice active listening and adapt your responses based on the dynamics of each interaction.

- Engage with people with varying backgrounds, perspectives, and communication preferences.

- Explore multiple formats, including one-on-one conversations, group discussions, debates, or presentations.

- Experiment with different nonverbal signals to convey empathy, confidence, or assertiveness, depending on the situation.

Consistently reflect on each of these conversations. Be attuned to those moments when you reach a state of focused abstraction, or alternatively, when your conversational partner does. I saw the power of this firsthand with one of the people I interviewed for this book, someone who seemed to demonstrate an amazing capacity for recognizing, diagnosing, and activating his gut feel.

This man was the driver who was hired to take me to the airport after I gave a keynote speech in Pittsburgh, Pennsylvania. We started chatting casually—I didn't intend to interview him for this book—and I discovered that his main job was running a carpet cleaning company. It was a lucrative business that brought in a high six-figure profit each year.

He told me how he had worked at a glass warehouse before working at a carpet cleaning company—because he had a gut feel. And how he started his own carpet cleaning company—because he had a gut feel that he could do it better.

He met his wife when he was still at the glass warehouse. She was working at a steel mill, the first woman to do so, he proudly told me. They didn't have a women's bathroom at this steel mill, so she had to walk across the street to use the women's bathroom in the glass warehouse. He saw her come in every time she used the bathroom. Each time, he had a gut feel. She was already engaged, but he just knew. He told me, "I had to be consistent, not persistent. I respected her and knew that I just needed to be who I was and trust in being consistently who I was, and that everything else would fall into place." He married her, and they have been together for forty-two years.

Story after story, he told me about situations where he had trusted his gut feel. It never led him astray.

I shared stories about my own life, my own dilemmas. I asked him what his gut feel was on a few tough decisions I was facing. He told me—and he was right.

I asked him why he was driving a limo. He said that he had good employees who kept his carpet-cleaning business running pretty smoothly. He picked the right people whom he had "a good feeling about." Plus, he liked driving limos on the side because he enjoyed "meeting lots of people." He gets to talk to "old people, VPs of companies, football players, superrich people."[*]

In case you're wondering, that gut feel that he had about the decision I was facing? It was related to taking on a lucrative project that I was uncertain about. After I explained the situation, he said, "The way I see it, I want to have enough money to be the same person I am. I think you're the same," he added with a quick glance at me. I felt a Jolt and turned down that project, leaving not only lots of money on the table, but many questions about why I would turn down such a desired, sought-after project[†] that could lead to a plethora of more opportunities in the future.[‡] I turned it down so that I could be the same person that I am—and it's one of the best decisions I've ever made.

Over time, I realized that this man's gut feel had been informed by meeting so many different people, hearing their stories and challenges, making observations, and gaining new perspectives. This exposure enhanced his awareness, fed his mental models, schemas, and prototypes, and enabled him to reach a state of focused abstraction. With intention and practice, we all can become more attuned in this way.

---

[*] "Who are miserable shells of people," he added.

[†] Except Justin Kan, who also gets it. He reminds us not to get trapped in our Zone of Excellence—the things you are great at but that sap your energy—because you will find yourself excelling at a job you hate. Instead, aspire to live in your Zone of Genius, the things you love doing that give you energy. Justin Kan (@justinkan): "Every founder should aspire to live in their Zone of Genius: the things you love doing that give you energy. Don't get trapped in your Zone of Excellence (the things you are great at but sap your energy). You will find yourself excelling at a job you hate," X, May 22, 2019, 10:36 a.m., https://x.com/justinkan/status/1131207138418630657.

[‡] You play silly games, you win silly prizes.

13

Prompted Action

If you listen carefully, you'll recognize prompts
that compel you to action.

better understanding of our personified, embodied, emotional, and cognitive gut feel gives us the foundation for honing our ability to recognize—and act on—the important inputs we receive that are prompting us to act. We know how our *own* Eureka, Spidey Sense, and Jolts might present and manifest, understand the significance and relevance of the prompts we receive, and improve our ability to get to a state of focused abstraction. We can create a tapestry of connections like Amanda did.

Amanda Phingbodhipakkiya* is an artist who said of her poignant portraits and murals, "I think people misunderstand my work sometimes—I use bright colors, vibrant imagery and my work is filled with hope, not because I'm trying to diminish the grief or the pain . . . but because we don't need to be reminded of what we

---

* Amanda's last name is Thai and is pronounced (PUNG-bodee-bak-ee-ah). It's a long last name. Her website? www.alonglastname.com.

experience on a daily basis." This formed part of her nomological network.

In 2022, she was painting a commissioned mural outside the US Embassy in Bangkok, Thailand, when she noticed an important prompt—one that changed the entire trajectory of her career. The prompt was subtle, something any of us could have ignored.

The US Ambassador to Thailand stopped by for a photo op. The photographers began clicking as he picked up a brush and started painting for a bit alongside Amanda. They started chatting informally. At one point, the ambassador mentioned how he wanted to "create a tapestry of connections." Amanda's ears perked up at the word *tapestry*. Hearing that word brought a quick moment of clarity and certainty, and with a feeling of excitement and energy, she described how she had a sudden gut feel and knew that she had to pitch him, right then and there.

Amanda's pitch—that bold stroke—led to what she called "the biggest and most meaningful project of her life." She said, "The perfect pitch just formulated, seemingly out of thin air, and within seconds."

Looking back, it seemed both vivid and memorable, but during that moment of pause, it felt ordinary. It's often like that. *The* moment that many of us have in our careers can be so ordinary that it just comes and goes, unheralded. It feels normal and commonplace, even though we recognize it as a special moment later on. When Mozart composed his music in a moment of flourish, he was almost blasé in its description: "Whence and how they come, I know not, nor can I force them." The same was true of Dirac for the moment he wrote his famous antimatter equations: "My equations were smarter than I was."

We often let these fleeting moments pass. We might notice a

prompt and feel the urge to act but don't. Amanda did. She had developed her ability to recognize and heed the prompt which brought her to a state of focused abstraction.

Amanda was raised in the United States, the daughter of Thai and Indonesian immigrants. Her art played a very dormant role in her world. Many times, she considered giving it up entirely and taking a more conventional job—until March 2020, when lockdown orders were issued in New York City to slow the spread of COVID-19.

Amanda was on the subway in New York City when the man next to her looked at her, said, "Ew, gross!" and ran to the other end of the car. A bit shaken, she continued to experience and observe egregious anti-Asian discrimination and harassment[*] in the months to come—something she had previously never encountered before in this city that she loved and considered home. It compelled her to create a series of portraits entitled *I Still Believe in Our City*.

Before pursuing a career in art, Amanda had majored in neuroscience at Columbia University. That training guided her. She had always been interested in research on how the human brain processes rejection. It formed part of her reasoned gut feel. It also helped her be in touch with her embodied gut feel. "When we are shunned or we feel isolated or alone, our bodies react as if we had experienced physical harm," she says. "My practice of making the invisible visible—whether it's microscopic worlds or the often unseen struggles of communities of color—comes from the same place of revealing the unsung or the unseen."

Her portraits of members of the AAPI community appeared in

---

[*] In fact, reports increased sevenfold between February and July 2020 and the same time frame in 2019.

Posters and mural at Atlantic Avenue-Barclays Center
subway station, New York City

Public billboard, New York City

subway stations, bus shelters, and other public places in New York
City at a time when reports of anti-Asian discrimination and ha-
rassment continued to rise. One portrait, entitled *With Softness and
Power*, graced the cover of *TIME* magazine's March 2021 issue.

This brought her name and her art into the public conversation,
and soon, rather than living the "struggling artist" existence, she
found herself being invited to art events and receiving commissions

We Are Tomorrow (2022). US Embassy, Bangkok, Thailand.
Acrylic latex on concrete. 9' x 42'

to paint murals and create installations. That led to the opportunity to paint the mural for the US Embassy in Bangkok, Thailand, the same one I mentioned at the opening of this chapter. The mural, which faces the street, depicts a group of bold women and nonbinary people inspired by the artist's conversations with those communities. It's a vision for Thai society that can be celebrated and championed by all.

As she explained this to Ambassador Robert Godec, he likened it to a "tapestry" and spoke of his desire to "create a tapestry of connections." She felt a feeling of "fit" between what she was hearing, her recollections of Godec speaking about it in previous remarks, and what she'd always felt internally. She had long been thinking about how to connect people and, for the past few years, about how to truly do so with her art.

This prompt, the word *tapestry*: "A tapestry is created by weaving colored threads through plain threads. The plain warp threads are stretched on a loom and act as a grid for weavers to create a pattern with the colored weft threads, allowing scenes to emerge—scenes that tell a story."

She immediately pitched Godec on an installation, a tapestry of sorts, that would bring together textiles from Thailand and the US. It would weave together—through her own long march—the historical, cultural, modern, and real stories of Thailand. It would tell the story of the traditions preserved by the local Thai communities and the everyday artisans who labor to create dyes from seaweed and from indigo in the forest. The idea just came to her—*whence and how it came, she knows not; her art was smarter than she was.*

In June 2023, Amanda traveled to Thailand to begin her research on this tapestry of connections. It is her most meaningful project yet.

US Ambassador to Thailand Robert F. Godec and Amanda Phingbodhipakkiya
Photo courtesy of Amanda Phingbodhipakkiya

We Live in a Network of Stories

We get better at taking action when we heed the prompts that come about over the course of our interactions and conversations with others.

Every person has a story. When you meet someone, listen to theirs. Try to find out what powers them, what keeps them going. Get to know them. What are the inflection points that have changed the course of their lives and made them who they are? People reveal themselves to you if you let them.

Ray Dalio, the billionaire founder of Bridgewater Associates, says that in any conversation, you can figure out the prompt or the core thread. It comes down to one simple question: "When you hear someone's description of what's happening, ask yourself: What are their biases and goals?"

This applies to everything, he says, whether you're asking for advice, in casual conversation, reading the newspaper, or watching the news. "Most people are trying to sell you something that will help them get the things they want," he adds, whether it is selling you on their ideas, advice, intelligence, or product or service.

I was thinking about what Dalio said as I was having lunch with Samantha, a popular congresswoman who had introduced numerous impactful bills and resolutions into legislation and was known for being a great advocate for the people in her district. She served on some of the most essential committees in the Senate and was well respected by her peers. After talking a bit about her job and her day-to-day responsibilities, we started chatting about her children, and I was riveted by what she told me.

When her two oldest children, both girls, were four years old and a year and a half, she became pregnant with her third, a son.

She was in her last trimester, but she and her family were given the green light to visit her in-laws in Australia. While there, her husband's grandfather, who lived in Brazil, had a life-threatening accident. Her husband and her father-in-law flew to Brazil to assist.* While they were in flight, Samantha went into labor, and her son was born—premature but healthy. Samantha gave birth in a foreign country, with an ob-gyn she had just met attending and with only her mother-in-law to help her (and her two daughters).

When her husband landed in Brazil, he learned of his son's birth. He made plans to quickly see his grandfather should this be his last time with him, assist in any way he could at the hospital, and help his father get settled so that his father could handle the rest without him—before returning to Australia. However, while on the flight back to Australia, their son, not quite two days old, died of an undiagnosed complication.

Samantha's story was deeply tragic, but it also had elements of joy, familial love, compassion, and benevolence. My heart went out to her, for all that she had been through. I was similarly moved. It's a story that resonated with so many people and so many of her constituents, and it's one of the reasons she was such a popular political figure. I offered her personal resources and introductions, provided her with help on an initiative, and sang her praises within my own network.

But. Two weeks later, Samantha's career was completely derailed, rocked with scandal on charges of nepotism, favoritism, and trading of favors for influence. She was called a social climber, a cheat, and a fake; people said that she had used her background story as virtue signaling.

---

* This was a family of public servants and government officials who were posted in the US and all over the world, including Australia and Brazil.

I thought back to my lunch with her. I recalled that as she told her story, she kept bringing up other people. She mentioned a famous politician numerous times, saying how he sent her a lavish gift basket after her son's death. She called this politician her "congressional brother." She referred to another politician as her "congressional mother." She mentioned a former White House executive who was also her "congressional mother," a famous lobbyist who was her "personal counselor," and another top leader who was her "congressional brother." There were so many names being dropped that it almost distracted from the story she was telling about her family.

Had I heeded these prompts, I would have noticed the display and emphasis that she put on titles, status, and reputational standing, and I would not have been so blindsided by her ultimate fall. She had been implicitly disclosing to me that, despite her strong emotional connection to people, she was driven by self-gain. It was a good lesson for me to pay attention, listen closely, and stay attuned to the people who come into my life.

Mastering Your Intuition

Exercise: Listen for the prompts that are
directing you toward action.

In all your conversations, notice:

1. **Themes:** Listen with the intent to understand your conversational partner's biases and goals. See if you can pinpoint them. What are the types of actions they are likely to impulsively initiate based on these perspectives?

2. **A different theme:** Listen for themes again, but this time, identify a different theme—maybe fear, love, and loss. There's a quote by H. Jackson Brown Jr., which reminds us to "remember that everyone you meet is afraid of something, loves something, and has lost something." See if you can determine what they fear, what they love, and a particular loss. What types of bold strokes would this lead them to undertake?

3. **Yet another theme:** It's your choice of theme. Maybe it's humor and solemnity (where do they feel light and where do they feel heavy?). Maybe it's kindness and firmness (where are they generous and open and where are they closed off and stern?). It doesn't matter what theme you focus on. What's important is that at the end of each of these conversations, you understand something core about the person—and about how it connects to you and your understanding of their world and the long march that they'd be willing to embark upon in their life journey.

4. **Repetition:** We often listen for what resonates with us, but we don't always listen for repetition. People repeat themselves, even when they're not using the same words or expressions verbatim. What ideas are they subtly repeating? What they repeat is what is most important to them and what they are most compelled to act upon.

5. **Keywords or cues:** When we are listening for keywords or cues, we are conversing in a way that allows us to go deeper, more biological even. The natural world often sends signals so salient that they can keep us from danger, like certain colorations* warning that a plant or ani-

---

* Scientifically called *aposematism*.

mal is poisonous (or at least distasteful). We notice how the rustling of a mouse as it forages in the undergrowth provides a cue conveying information to a predator about the mouse's location* and the actions they'd take as a result.

6. **Coincidences:** Is there anything that is said during the conversation that seems uncanny, that is related to something you've been thinking or grappling with, and is just too close to ignore?

7. **Interruptions:** Listen by interrupting. Yup, you read that right. I know that we were taught not to interrupt. But this time, interrupt. Not in an impatient, self-important way that signals that you think what you have to say is more important than what you are hearing. You're interrupting with purpose by asking questions to get more details and nuances that might be relevant. Gently probe by asking, "And then what happened?" or "And then what did you do?" You're politely asking questions and seeking to learn more in an empathetic manner.

Practice these listening skills in all your conversations. Try a different one each day. For example, today, all conversations are about listening for repetition, no matter who you're talking to; tomorrow, all conversations are about listening for coincidences.

As we hone these listening skills, we'll get better at recognizing the prompts that are directing us toward action. We'll begin to

---

* Yes, the information from this cue is more indirect. Sometimes we have to do some processing and intuiting to even sense certain cues. The rustling cues are purely a by-product of the mouse's foraging activity and the information that it conveys can be misconstrued, misinterpreted, or ignored entirely. In contrast, signals like colorism are more direct and have the specific purpose of conveying information, thereby influencing behavior (in the case of aposematism, it has directly been shaped by natural selection to impact both the signaler's and the recipient's fitness).

trust that the signals we notice, for example, are fundamentally informative, providing us with useful information that gives us a gut feel we can trust and helps us choose the right response.

Gut feel moments come from what we already know.* Anne Morrow Lindbergh once said, "Good conversation is as stimulating as black coffee, and just as hard to sleep after." That's because listening as we're conversing enables us to recognize prompts that compel us to take action through those bold strokes and long marches.

---

* Even Jolts because they mark a shift from what we know.

Iterations

14

The Relevance of Experience

What is most challenging to learn are the things
we think we already know.

It's true that you should always learn from experience, but ask yourself: Do you have twenty years of experience, or is it more like one year of experience repeated twenty times?

Ron Johnson was chosen to be the new CEO of JCPenney on November 2011. There was immense excitement and anticipation surrounding his appointment. Johnson was highly regarded in the retail industry for his successful tenure at both Target and Apple, where he played a pivotal role in shaping and developing retail strategy. He was seen as someone who would bring fresh ideas, innovation, and a renewed sense of direction to the struggling department store chain. He had a reputation for being a retail visionary, who could revitalize brands and drive growth in sales and profitability.

Johnson came in with ambitious plans to overhaul JCPenney's pricing strategy, store layout, and merchandise assortment. His vision for a "fair and square" pricing model and a more modern, engaging shopping experience resonated with the board members who hired him. After all, at Target, he was one of the key individuals responsible for developing partnerships with designers and brands to create exclusive, stylish, and affordable collections. This strategy helped Target differentiate itself from its competitors and attract a more design-conscious customer base. It was because of Johnson that Target became known informally as "Tar-gét" or "Tar-zhay."

Similarly, at Apple, he created the Apple store experience that we know today. He played a central role in designing the store layout, customer service approach, and overall experience. He invented the Genius Bar, where customers could receive personalized assistance and technical support. His vision for a space where customers could not only buy products but also experience them, led to minimalist, aesthetically pleasing designs that enabled customers to try out products, attend workshops, and receive expert advice. Apple Stores became iconic, generating tremendously high sales per square foot and serving as a model for retail innovation in consumer companies.

It was assumed that Johnson would turn JCPenney into a similar success story. What happened, however, was quite the opposite. In April 2013, less than eighteen months after he was hired, he was fired—and his tenure at the company deemed the "biggest business failure of the 21st century."

What happened? Johnson fell prey to his situational arrogance.

Never Become Such an Expert that You Stop Learning

Voltaire once said that "doubt is an uncomfortable condition, but certainty is a ridiculous one."

Situational arrogance is a context-specific mindset where individuals rely on (what they believe is) their gut feel and have an erroneous sense of confidence and superiority in particular situations or circumstances. This most often emerges when individuals perceive themselves as having highly competent, knowledgeable, or successful schemas, mental models, and prototypes, leading them to ignore the prompts that might point them to a different intuition.

The most common reason why individuals fall prey to situational arrogance is because they have achieved a high level of expertise or success in a particular domain. Once our minds slip into this state, it takes a great deal of agility to override. That is why specialists are often the last ones to recognize commonsense solutions to problems, a limitation economist Thorstein Veblen calls the "trained incapacity" of experts.*

It happens often. Here's an everyday example: How many times have we received the check at the end of a meal and been shocked that the bill was so high—or so much lower than we had expected? We can practice reining it in by "answering the questions first" ("What am I predicting the amount of this bill will be?") so that we can see if we are surprised by the answer ("My sense for costs fails tremendously when I'm in a new country or when I am the one choosing the wine from the cellar").

Similarly, perhaps we assume that a dish will turn out better than it did when we made some adjustments to the recipe. Maybe we underestimate the time it takes to travel to a destination because we didn't anticipate that there would be traffic congestion or bridge closures. Or perhaps we assume that we know how a friend or family

---

* One trick Thomas Edison used to overcome this problem was to give problems to people who had the "wrong" expertise, after people with the "right" expertise had failed to solve them—in the same vein as the neuroplasticity exercises that we discussed earlier in the Mastering Your Intuition Exercise in chapter 13.

member will react in a given situation, but we find that there were much larger conflicts, misunderstandings, and hurt feelings than we'd expected.

When Ron Johnson introduced the "Fair and Square" pricing strategy, he already had a prototype on consistent, set prices—something that worked well for him at Apple. He aimed to eliminate the use of constant sales and discounts and instead offer everyday low prices. It was not well received by JCPenney's customer base, however, which had become accustomed to sales and coupon-driven shopping. Its traditional customers, who were looking for deals and discounts, were alienated by the new pricing strategy. Sales plummeted as loyal customers left, and the company struggled to attract new ones.

When Johnson implemented a store layout change, he did so again based on his tremendous success at Target and Apple, converting the traditional store-within-a-store concept into a more open layout. This move at JCPenney, however, disrupted the familiar shopping experience for JCPenney customers, causing confusion and frustration.

Each of these changes led to a decline in morale among JCPenney employees. The company's long-standing culture was disrupted, which affected employee engagement and performance. It was Johnson's reliance on his successful experiences at Target and Apple that led him to make critical mistakes—applying strategies that worked well previously to a situation that he didn't realize was overwhelmingly different. He went from innovative brands to a traditional department store with a different customer base and expectations. His failure to understand and adapt to the unique dynamics of JCPenney's market and customers ultimately led to significant financial losses and his departure from the company.

Gut feel is informed by experience, but it can be hampered by situational arrogance during our intuiting process. Johnson's situational arrogance blinded him to his new context and the variables that came with it.*

We can draw from our experiences while reigning in our situational arrogance to sharpen our intuition and gut feel.

Mastering Your Intuition

Exercise: Understand your own experiences
from the lives of others.

One of the most effective ways to learn from our experiences is, surprisingly, by getting away from them, so that we can later place them in the proper context.

It's been said that fiction is a lie that tells us true things, over and over. Reading fiction enables us to inhabit the minds of other people and see the world through their eyes. Works of nonfiction can accomplish the same when they are not limited to the highly technical, instructional, explanatory, and report-based recounting, and instead are more opinion-based and persuasive. It's especially apparent in memoirs and philosophical works. We can inhabit the minds of others and see through their eyes. Even a straightforward biography of Cleopatra or a history of World War II might make us wonder: What would we have done in Cleopatra's shoes? Or in Neville Chamberlain's?

Read a lot, and then reflect on your own life through the prism of literary themes, ideas, and characters. Your own beliefs, values,

---

* You change one variable and everything changes. First rule of Fight Club—and algebra.

and experiences are never far away, even when you're immersed in a book. You are always introspecting, self-examining, and drawing connections—absorbing new insights into yourself in relation to the world.

Seeing yourself in situations you've never been in and observing protagonists in situations you're familiar with helps you better understand your experiences and be attuned to your gut feel. It also gives you deeper grounding and greater perspective. You begin to build into your schemas, mental models, and prototypes the recognition that the world is complex and uncertain—because the challenges that protagonists face are inherently complex or chaotic problems—and you intuitively stay open to the possibility of uncertainty, with the willingness to adapt to changing circumstances.

Pick a book to read. If you don't know where to start, take a look in appendix A, where I provide a few suggestions. Note that this is not necessarily a list of my favorites—different works speak to us in different ways. This is the point: If we all read the same things, we're all going to have the same thoughts and mental models. So, read broadly. My list is more broad than deep.

As you're reading, bookmark or dog-ear* each page with a section or phrase that resonates with you. When you've finished the book, write a very simple book report. It can be as long or as short as you'd like—don't make this homework for yourself. I use a template that looks roughly like this:

---

* I always read physical books. I just don't get the same experience otherwise. Whatever format you choose is fine. I know dog-earing (also known as page-folding and corner-turning) is considered blasphemous by many readers. I actually dog-ear the bottom corners of the book (as if that makes it better), but you can use Post-it notes or other types of bookmarks if you prefer. For a history of dog-earing, see Torsten Landsberg, "The History of the Dog-Ear Bookmark," *DW*, April 23, 2021, https://dw.com/en/world-book-day-history-of -the-dog-ear-bookmark/a-57311160.

Title: _____

Date: _____

Author: _____

Book rating: _____

Overall thoughts:

Notable excerpts:

I go back to the book and transcribe all the quotes and excerpts on the pages that I'd dog-eared. Sometimes I include some of my own thoughts or reflections after the quote (which I indicate with brackets). Afterward, I summarize my overall thoughts in a few sentences. I find that this allows me to reread the entire book quickly, focusing on just the parts that resonated with me, which gives me a better sense of how the book applies to my own life and to the world around me.

For example, a book titled *Tomorrow, and Tomorrow, and Tomorrow* made me aware of my situational arrogance and rethink a career decision that I had been struggling with but knew was wrong. I'd noted down this quote:

> He had begun to suspect that while he had an obvious aptitude for math, he was not particularly inspired by it. . . . "You're incredibly gifted, Sam," his professor said. "But it is worth noting that to be good at something is not quite the same as loving it."

It made me realize that although I had gotten extremely profi-
cient in a career in investment banking, it wasn't something that
allowed me to provide value in a way that would sustain me long
term. I didn't love it.

After completing a few reflective reports (appendix B is a sam-
ple), try adding a degree of difficulty. Do this exercise with books
that you've read in the past. Ursula Le Guin once said, "If a book
told you something when you were fifteen, it will tell you it again
when you're fifty, though you may understand it so differently that
it seems you're reading a whole new book."

I recently reread Edith Wharton's book *Ethan Frome*. I noticed
that this book was different from Edith Wharton's other works:
While the characters in her other books belonged to the upper
class, those in *Ethan Frome* did not. Despite that, all of Wharton's
characters faced the same dilemma—whether to fulfill their duty
or follow their heart. Rereading it decades later affirmed my sentiment that the suffering endured by her characters seemed exces-
sive, unjustified, and almost cruel, but now I also saw how it provided
a commentary on how the American economic and cultural systems produce and allow such suffering.

Don't shy away from young adult or children's books. There are
so many profound themes in these volumes, and many of them will
resonate in ways that you don't expect.

With these reflective reports, you'll have a "library of refer-
ences" that you can draw from. Like Adam in an earlier chapter,
find the one that fits your situation and take it down to use at that
moment. Apply what is most relevant for the problem that you're
trying to solve.

15

The Value of Mistakes

*Make bold choices. Some may turn out
to be mistakes. They all add up to
the person you become.*

Ron Johnson made a mistake at JCPenney. But he also made huge progress in developing his intuition and his gut feel. I have no doubt that Johnson will see many more successes in his life, successes of the magnitude of what he accomplished at Apple and Target. It's not unlike learning to cook. You're going to burn a few pans and over-salt a few sauces—but over time, you'll start to master the flavors, timing, and techniques. Mistakes and failure help us build our schemas, mental models, and prototypes. So even when you're getting it "wrong" about certain people or decisions, you're developing your gut feel.

This is important because industries transform, the nature of business itself will evolve, and the considerations of leaders and managers will change. Making decisions that were once deemed "correct," according to formerly accepted norms, will become mistakes that we'll need our intuition to understand, and our gut feel to help us correct. Jensen Huang, the co-founder and CEO of NVIDIA, who transformed his company into a dominant force in the tech industry, driving innovations that revolutionized gaming, AI, data processing, and autonomous vehicle technologies, attested to this: "If you work in a very technology-driven industry, it is essential that you understand the underpinnings of the technology so that you have an intuition for how the industry is going to change and the mistakes that will be made. You need to have an intuition for which one of the technologies is a bit of left turn and which one is fundamental."

Intrapersonal Mistakes

There are mistakes that we make that are "self-related," mistakes arising from internal misjudgments, choices, or actions. These provide us with insights into personal growth and enhance our self-awareness. Perhaps we remember a time when we've taken on too much, for example, and that feeling of being overwhelmed leads us to a breaking point that forces us to reassess our limits. This mistake teaches us the importance of saying no and prioritizing. We learn important lessons about our personal boundaries, time management, and what truly matters to us.

Dozens of people I interviewed for this book shared stories of starting businesses and founding start-ups, later realizing that it was a mistake and they shouldn't have done so. Many have also shared stories of staying in jobs when they should have taken a chance and started their business. So I asked, how do you know when it's the right time to start a business? My favorite answer was from the founder of Farmgirl Flowers, who said "There was something telling me that I couldn't *not* start this business. I just had to do it."

Mistakes happened when individuals ignored their history and what they really cared about deep down, so it's extremely important to learn the importance and consequences of pursing (mis) aligned goals. One way that I teach this to my students is by asking them to engage in an exercise that helps them to think about their goals, timing, boundaries, and bold ideas, all at the same time, integrating their priors and prompts. Let me walk you through it.

Spend a specific amount of time—it can be two days, three months, or any duration you want to set for yourself—to wildly brainstorm. Keep a notebook handy, so you can capture any and all ideas for a business, start-up venture, product, or service that would allow you to create value (profit value or social value). Continue to jot down all ideas that come to mind during this set time period. Don't think about any boundaries, constraints, or risks at all.

Once you've done this, you're likely to have a pretty long list of ideas. Now put this list aside. Do not think about anything on that list. Grab a different notebook and start writing down all the relevant characteristics and attributes of you and your life, as they apply to work and starting a business. For example, you might write:

- I hate working with people. (Or: I'm a people person and love networking and interacting with others.)

- I don't want a company that will rely on social media for customers and marketing.

- I want a company where I don't have to be working 24/7; I want to be able to just put in a solid eight hours a day and be done.

- I want to have a family, and it's important that I'm able to spend lots of quality time with my children.

And so on. Remember, don't think about any of the ideas that you wrote down in the first notebook.

When you've finished writing down all the parameters you can think of, take your list of business ideas and ruthlessly cross out any idea that does not align with *every single one* of your parameters. It doesn't matter how in love with a business idea you are. Cross it off if it does not align. Once you're through with this part of the exercise, you're usually left with just three to five business ideas. Start testing each of them to see which will actually stick.

The beauty of this exercise is that it forces you to "see" mistakes. As you cross things out—especially ideas you might be enamored with—you'll see how they might just be fads, or perhaps an excellent idea, but just not an excellent idea for *you*. You start to understand which goals (or people)* may be misaligned with your true passions or values, so you don't make those mistakes. Knowing this helps you refocus on what brings you genuine fulfillment and happiness.

---

* Often, pursuing the wrong people can be even more damaging than pursuing the wrong business. Many entrepreneurs told me that they "didn't listen to their gut and signed up with the wrong investors and venture capitalists." One shared how "in the eleventh hour, they asked me to fire someone, asked me about student loans, made me cry, grilled me on my spending habits, asked to speak directly with clients, and altogether turned everything into a failure on my behalf." Another shared how picking the wrong investor led to financial ruin. This entrepreneur, who came from humble beginnings, started a company that became very successful and received an acquisition offer of $30 million just eighteen months after founding his business. He was ready to make the deal, wanting nothing more than to use part of his earnings to buy his mother a house. The investor, who at this point had majority control of the company, refused to let him accept the offer, going so far as to say, "Thirty million dollars? Is that even money? You're not selling this company until it's worth at least three hundred million dollars." Over the next two years, the founder faced tremendous risk and competitive dynamics, and his business went bankrupt.

Interpersonal Mistakes

While some mistakes are intrapersonal, there are those that we make over the course of our interactions with others. Interpersonal mistakes impact our understanding of and our relationships and communications with others. We might, for example, misjudge another person or their intentions (or be the recipient of another's erroneous judgments). We might be overly critical of others (or be the recipient of others' criticism). Making interpersonal mistakes help us learn valuable lessons about trust, empathy, and reading social cues. They lead us to reflect on our assumptions and biases, encouraging better communication and understanding in the future.

Cam shared a story that has stayed with me and that I think about often. In the early part of his career, he was a senior director at a renowned family foundation that made philanthropic donations worth millions of dollars. His job was to evaluate and fund projects that were meant to improve social welfare and economic prosperity across the world. As you can imagine, he was extremely well-connected, and he had people requesting to meet with him on a daily basis. He loved meeting people, hearing their ideas, and forming strong friendships with many of the recipients he had funded.

A few years ago, Cam left the foundation. Taking a chance on himself, he decided to work on his own passion project. He started reaching out to some of his contacts, telling them that he'd love to talk with them about his new work and get their thoughts. One of these contacts, a woman he had awarded a number of large grants to through the years, had become a close friend and trusted confidante—or so he thought.

He sent her an email, letting her know that he had left the

foundation and was working on some independent projects outside of the philanthropic world. A few weeks passed without a response. This woman was normally very responsive, and he knew that she was still actively running projects and attending industry events, so Cam sent a follow-up email: "You may have gotten busy, but was wondering if you saw my last message. . . . Would love to chat and get your thoughts. . . ."

Another month went by. Radio silence. He decided to send one more email: "Look, I won't bother you again, but if you'd like to chat . . ."

She finally responded with a Calendly link* and a one-line message: "Let's meet for 30 minutes sometime in February when things are less busy." It was July.

Cam talks about those three years of working on his passion project as one of the darkest periods in his life. He learned hard lessons about the transactional nature of many of his "friendships." These painful experiences taught him tremendously valuable skills involving perception, attribution, and discernment. He became a better judge of character.

Last year, Cam became one of the top five executives at a global media company known for its influential business publications—and its lists, such as the 40 Under 40 list of the most influential leaders, innovators, and entrepreneurs under the age of forty. He is personally responsible for seeking out and recognizing rising talent,

---

* A scheduling platform that automates online appointment bookings. The tool simplifies the process of booking meetings by allowing users to share their availability through a personalized link. When you receive a Calendly link, you click on it to view the sender's free time slots. You simply select a time that works for you, provide the necessary details (such as your name and email), and confirm the meeting. The appointment is then automatically added to both your calendar and the sender's—and notifications and reminders are sent—without the back-and-forth of traditional scheduling.

curating the lists to showcase individuals who are shaping the future of business, culture, and technology. About a month after starting this position, he received an email from his Calendly link contact: "I just heard about your new role! Congratulations, my friend. . . . Let's catch up. Would love to tell you about what I've been working on."

Cam deleted the email. A few weeks later, he received another: "You may have gotten busy, but was wondering if you saw my last message. . . . Would love to chat and get your thoughts."

Another month passed, and he received yet another email: "Look, I won't bother you again, but if you'd like to chat . . ." He told me that he would have just deleted that one as well, if it weren't for a line that caught his eye: "I guess you've forgotten about me, now that you're in this new role."

He responded, "I didn't forget about you. I just didn't forget that you forgot about me."

Cam's twenty-five years of experience with global corporate, government, and philanthropic organizations has made him passionate about the ways leaders apply optimistic and inclusive solutions to their most difficult challenges. But his twenty-five years of experience have also helped him master his intuition. He shared: "Developing intuition is what I imagine learning to ride a skateboard is like. We have to fall sometimes to get good at it. So even in the getting it 'wrong' about certain people decisions, I was developing my instincts. Once I learned this, it made it easier to forgive myself for allowing certain elements into my life. As long as my instincts got better because of it, it was worth it."

Mastering Your Intuition

Exercise: Understand that mistakes and
misinterpretations happen—and allow for that.

We've heard of the 80/20 rule (the Pareto principle: 80 percent of
your results come from 20 percent of your efforts) and the advice to
figure out the right areas to focus on and make that your priority.
I've repurposed the Pareto principle into a rule I'm even more fond
of: Things will go wrong in my life 20 percent of the time. Let me
explain.

When things go wrong, there's this letdown that we experience because we somehow expected it to go right. But if we ask
ourselves, truly, "What percent of the time do you think things are
going to go wrong in your life?" Maybe 10 percent or 20 percent?
Maybe more? (I decided that my figure is 20 percent.) So now, when
things go wrong (and they inevitably will), instead of dwelling on it
or letting yourself feel too bad about it, just throw it in* that 20 percent bucket and appreciate it for what it is—an opportunity to master your intuition.

How? When we fail or something goes wrong, review the
type of problem it was and its specific context. This will help us
understand the sequence of events leading up to and following the
incident, including any triggers, actions taken, and outcomes. Analyzing the timeline establishes context and enables us to identify
critical moments that produced the result. This review also re-
veals the underlying causes of the problem, including systemic issues, process failures, human errors, technical limitations, as well
as any contributing factors like communication breakdowns, re-

---

* Obviously, this is not meant to apply to or make light of truly serious situations, such as
death, sickness, and other disasters.

source constraints, and external dependencies that may have played a role. We can evaluate the decision-making process along the way, assessing the prompts and priors and whether there were any assumptions.

Finally, it reminds us to run more "failed" experiments and to pressure test. Noting that things just aren't going to go our way 20 percent of the time (or more) takes some of the sting out of making mistakes. It helps us build resilience by learning to view mistakes as opportunities for growth where we can conduct "postmortems."* You'll embrace challenges and setbacks as a normal part of the learning process more readily, bounce back from adversity, and become mentally stronger. Failed experiments will also temper your situational arrogance. Mistakes humble you by reminding you of your fallibility and the limitations of your expertise. You'll be prompted to explore alternative solutions and approaches that you might not have considered otherwise, sparking creativity and innovation.

Additionally, we can also quantify how long you can feel terrible, depending on how badly something went wrong.† I might decide, for instance, that something was "two hours bad" or "one day bad" or "one week bad." That's the amount of time that I give myself to be sad or angry or indulge in chocolate binges to make myself feel better. But when that time is up, then I need to move forward and take action. Instead of wallowing in my feelings and letting my mistakes gnaw at me, little by little, I allow them to inform my schemas, mental models and prototypes productively.

Once you've gone through this exercise of writing down some of your mistakes, you'll be able to connect the dots between them. Look for patterns and make adjustments. That's how you get better.

---

* In the workplace, conducting project postmortems are processes that allow individuals, teams, and other stakeholders review and evaluate the results at the end of the project or after the resolution of an incident.

† Again, this does not apply to life-and-death problems.

1. What was the context?

2. What was the timeline leading up to it?

3. What were the associated factors?

4. What prompts, priors, or assumptions were involved?

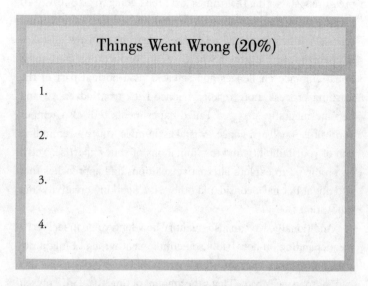

Things Went Wrong (20%)

1.

2.

3.

4.

Things Went Right (80%)

1.

2.

3.

4.

Once I learned and acknowledged the role my mistakes play in the development of my intuition, it made my failures easier to forgive. As long as my gut feel improved as a result, it was worth it in the long term. We're all going to make mistakes, and we're all going to fail, but we can learn how to fail well, so that we can hone our intuition and gut feel in the process.

Mary Tyler Moore once said, "You can't be brave if you've only had wonderful things happen to you." Be brave—and use your mistakes to master your gut feel.

Deploy Your Superpower

*Success is about deciding and acting on what
matters. Master your intuition and trust your
gut to lead you in the right direction.*

O n the last day of class, at the end of every course I teach, I conclude by giving my students* one last nugget of hard-earned wisdom. I tell them:

The difference between success and failure is seeing the endless subtle distinctions between the things that matter, the things that are supposed to matter but don't, and the things that may or may not matter, depending on other factors.

It's not the most profound statement they'll ever hear. Neither is it the most empowering one that I've said to them over the course of our time together. It's somewhat ambiguous, confusing, even. But so is life.

Einstein once said, "Before you listen to your head or your heart,

---

* By my last count, I've taught more than four thousand students at this point in my career.

decide first whether you have a better head or a better heart." When it comes to our intuition, we don't have to make this decision because our gut feel draws on both our head *and* our heart, the data *and* our experience, the prompts *and* our priors—*together*. It helps us decide what matters.

Data and intuition are often perceived as opposing forces in decision-making: data being objective, quantitative information, while intuition is subjective judgment based on feelings and instincts. However, as we've learned, data plays a significant role in informing and shaping gut feel through the intuiting process. We've seen how gut feel is influenced by all our priors stored in our (subconscious) mind. This includes data points and observations that we may not consciously be aware of but that we've absorbed over time.

During our intuiting process we recognize patterns and make subconscious connections between disparate pieces of information, like the connection between tomato sauce and Michelin-starred restaurants, or Post-it notes and pop-up ads. Data serves as the raw material for this pattern recognition process. When we encounter novel situations and receive new prompts, our gut feel is informed by past experiences and data points that resonate with our current scenario. We use data to supplement and validate our gut feel, providing additional evidence or context to support our decisions.

The beauty of our intuiting process is that it mines the entirety of our lived experience and draws on what we already know and what we didn't even realize we knew to produce a gut feel. As such, your gut feel *is* you. A superpower that is our very own, a gift unique to each of us.

Bushnell's law, or Nolan's law, is an aphorism often attributed to Atari founder Nolan Bushnell, who said about video game design: "All the best games are easy to learn and difficult to master."

The same is true of intuition. Throughout this book, I've tried to describe it and explain it as best I can. But intuition is like love, or cooking or chess or music. You can understand it and enjoy it at any level, but to truly master it is transcendent.

I've written this book to provide an actionable model to empower you to master your intuition so you're able to harness it intentionally. Rather than experiencing the intuiting process and the flash of clarity that is gut feel passively, as a spontaneous moment or a random occurrence that comes out of the blue, you can apply what you've learned in this book to proactively leverage your intuition to make the right decisions, take action, and solve your biggest problems. Through purposeful practice, you can develop it to deliver increasingly reliable signals, while heightening your own sensitivity to these signals, enabling you to act on those intuitive decisions with confidence—and do what truly matters.

Gut feel is you, and it whispers to you through your intuition. Be true to yourself and to that moment of clarity when your head and your heart converge. As the external world gets ever noisier, often, the smartest thing you can do is listen to your gut to guide you in the right direction. Trust yourself. You already know.

Acknowledgments

Writing this second book has been more challenging than I anticipated. Unlike the first, where ideas flowed effortlessly and I operated with fresh-eyed, unfiltered optimism, this book demanded something deeper. It required introspection, resolve, and a willingness to wrestle with the nuances that experience brings. Revisiting the foundations of my early work on gut feel, I was reminded of that raw, unguarded enthusiasm I once carried—untouched by the complexities of growth. This book, a return to those roots, became a reckoning with the learned knowledge that time inevitably delivers.

I am deeply grateful to those who have shaped and expanded my mental models, schemas, and prototypes, those who pushed me further and helped me hone my personified, embodied, emotional, and cognitive gut feel while I was writing this book.

To Faith Hamlin, who continued to have unwavering faith in me and in this project, and to Abigail Frank, not only for your detailed feedback on both books but for generously entertaining the side ideas I've thrown your way.

To the team at Portfolio, especially Casey Ebro, whose enthusiasm for this book never waned. To Leila Sandlin, for great feedback and help with securing rights; Niki Papadopoulos, for inspiring the title and ensuring smooth editorial transitions; and Adrian Zackheim, for his leadership and support in bringing this book to life. Thanks also to Kirstin Berndt, Jackie Galindo, Ritsuko Okumura, and Andrew Dudley and the entire sales team. I'm so grateful for all your efforts.

To Merry Sun, for believing in me, again, and to Eric Nelson, for giving me my start on this journey and always keeping it brutally honest.

To my Lavin family: Charles, for his friendship, generosity, and creative brilliance; Katy, for making the intro; to all the agents, especially Ken, Cathy, Tom, and Eliot; and David, for creating a special place for all those ideas.

To my DMSB and NEU family: my colleagues, collaborators, and fellow cabinet members, and DDC, a leader who has my back—something that I'll always appreciate.

To Jone, Port, Christine, and Robin, for their support of the research that sparked this book.

To Joan Lau, whose insights on the difference between gut feel and intuition were critical.

To Andy Wu, who is not only my go-to for Bayesian stats and priors and prompts, but also the first person I go to when there's a new conspiracy theory to take on.

To Tina Seelig, whose grace and graciousness have stayed with me from my first book to the writing of this second one.

To my Taiwan Taste-Off family and my Quads in Play crew (all you need is a chip and a chair), especially Kathy Cheng, Tait Sye, Cathy Hwang, Miles Hu, Lauren Chiang, Michael Chang, Stephanie Yang, and Mai Bach, for their feedback on everything from initial ideas to final cover designs, while also managing to refine my taste buds and my betting skills in the process.

To many trusted friends who provided invaluable feedback on various parts of this book and conversations of support along the way, especially Erin Earley, Ellen Wu, Marina Kishkovich, Liz Kwo, Ani Ross Grubb, Bruce Brownstein, LT Zhang, Zhenyu Liao, Patrick Lin, my Duke girls, Amit Shah, Chris Evdemon, Carey Lai, Mitch Joel, Laura Gassner Otting, Jerry Won, Anne Oliver, Andrew Chau, and Andrew Tratz and Joyce Chen (these two for also giving me their lake house when I needed peace to reflect and push through the final stages).

To those who have held a special place in my learning journey, including Benz and Li Jie, Raffi and Mac, Carrie Knerr O'Brien, Fen Kung, Georgia Lazana, Chi Cheng, and Than Phan Van.

To my students—those I've taught in 801, LEAD, Founder's Journey, ORGB, EDEN—who have been part of all the classroom discussions that have been so meaningful to me and inspired so much of this book.

To all those who were interviewed for this book and generously gave their time, especially those who were among the first to jump in and generously lend their insights, Amanda Phingbodhipakkiya, Jason Shen, and Dan Giusti.

To Chris and Mary (and J and R), who already knew. Hey, it's a gut feel.

To Mama, no, you can't help me write this book. But you already knew that.

To Ant, who already knows me more than I'd ever like to admit.

And finally, to L and A, who I hope already know that it was *they* who gave me life.

Appendix A

Recommended Titles

FICTION

Ethan Frome by Edith Wharton

Never Let Me Go by Kazuo Ishiguro

Because of Winn-Dixie by Kate DiCamillo

The Magic Strings of Frankie Presto by Mitch Albom

Love Story by Erich Segal

Our Town by Thornton Wilder

Americanah by Chimamanda Ngozi Adichie

Rosencrantz and Guildenstern Are Dead by Tom Stoppard

Inside Out and Back Again by Thanhha Lai

When the Legends Die by Hal Borland

Waiting for Godot by Samuel Beckett

Flowers for Algernon by Daniel Keyes

NONFICTION

When Breath Becomes Air by Paul Kalanithi

The Art of War by Sun Tzu

Big Magic by Elizabeth Gilbert

Uncultured by Daniella Mestyanek Young

The Book of Joy by His Holiness the Dalai Lama, Archbishop Desmond Tutu, and Douglas Abrams

Tender Bar by J. R. Moehringer

Sapiens by Yuval Noah Harari

Mythology by Edith Hamilton

How to Win Friends and Influence People by Dale Carnegie

Mandela by Anthony Sampson

The Rape of Nanking by Iris Chang

Edge by Laura Huang

Appendix B

Sample Reflective Book Report

Notes from *Lessons in Chemistry* by Bonnie Garmus
Read in late April to early May 2023. Finished on May 11, 2023.

This was another book that had a lot of hype around it. People raved about this book; people called it the best book they read this year.

I liked it. I thought it was really, really good. I thought it had good pacing, good elements of surprise, good narrative flow. It was good writing. There are a few nitpicky things that I had about it (I think I'll always have this, just because I'm such a perfectionist), but overall, really, really good.

I give the book a 9 out of 10. Very, very good. But I didn't sit unchanged after reading it. I didn't feel overcome with any emotion—regret, guilt, redemption, etc.

What I didn't like:

- I didn't like that one of the last scenes ended with the main character saying, "Class dismissed." That was stolen from the last line of *Boy Meets World*.

- I didn't like how heavy-handed the focus on feminism and equal rights and unfairness toward women at the hands of men was. But I'm not sure how the book would have worked, entirely, without that thesis.

What I thought was the most substantive parts of the book:

- This notion about "unfair share of happiness." I've been thinking a lot about envy and jealousy and have been much more balanced and at peace with being happy for others' success (after reading the *Book of Joy*, which discussed how everyone is striving. . . . "Good for you on achieving what you set out as a goal"; "Good for you for getting it"). People are inherently "self"-centered, and I like how I've been seeing broader than that recently.

- Second, was this notion in believing in ourselves. Too often, we hide behind reassurances. But change is necessary and good and deserving of being embraced. It takes courage to change. But with this courage and with this change and with this belief in yourself, you're unstoppable in the long run.

Excerpts from the book that I wanted to note down:

- His main issue was inexperience. He was like a dog who, after years of trying, catches a squirrel and then has absolutely no idea what to do with it. (p. 10)

- "Look, he said, life has never been fair, and yet you continue to operate as if it is—as if once you get a few wrongs straightened out, everything else will fall into place. They won't. You want my advice?" And before she could say no, he added, "Don't work the system. Outsmart it." (p. 26)

  - She sat silently, weighing his words. They made annoying sense in a terribly unfair way.

- "One thing I've learned: people will always yearn for a simple solution to their complicated problems. It's a lot easier to have faith in something you can't see, can't touch, can't explain, and can't change, rather than to have faith in something you actually can." She sighed. "One's self, I mean." (p. 39)

- When one is raised on a steady diet of sorrow, it's hard to imagine that others might have had an even larger serving. (p. 39)

- There's nothing more irritating than witnessing someone else's unfair share of happiness, and to some of their colleagues at Hastings Research Institute, Elizabeth and Calvin had an unfair share. He, because he was brilliant; she, because she was beautiful. When they became a couple, their unfair shares automatically doubled, making it really unfair. (p. 41)

  - The worst part, according to these people, was that they hadn't earned their shares—they'd simply been born that way, meaning their unfair share of happiness arose, not from hard work, but from (genetic) luck.

  - [And yet, people didn't know about the tragedies and hardship they had faced. . . . Calvin at the orphanage, Elizabeth with her family circumstances, etc.]

  - [Also, it's the same reason why people like to see academics giving up their lives, working to the bone, ruining their marriages. . . . It's like you sacrificed. . . . You earned your share. What HBS didn't like is that it seemed to come too naturally to me.]

- Physical suffering, he'd long ago learned, bonds people in a way that everyday life can't. (p. 46)

- Animals did this too, but with far more efficiency. Humans, Six-Thirty noticed, had a tendency to overcomplicate. (p. 59)

- She didn't want to admit it, but his words were like fresh fuel to her ever-growing pyre of self-doubt. She had neither the education nor the experience of the others. She not only lacked their credentials but their papers, peer support, financial backing, and awards. And yet, she knew—she *knew*—she was onto something. Some people were born to things; she was one of those people. (p. 72)

- No surprise. Idiots make it into every company. They tend to interview well. (p. 111)

- You'd be surprised how much you can tell about a baby at this stage, Mason was saying. They constantly reveal their future selves in the smallest of ways. (p. 162).

  - This one; she can read a room.

  - [I saw this with L, at two days old. His determination, his goal.]

- Actually, when you think about it, rowing is almost exactly like raising kids. Both require patience, endurance, strength, and commitment. And neither allow us to see where we're going—only where we've been. (p. 166)

  - (You row backwards, so you can't see where you're going, but you can see where you've been.)

- On the other hand, wasn't that the very definition of life? Constant adaptations brought about by a series of never-ending mistakes? (p. 169)

- . . . How Mad could sense exactly those things everyone wanted to hide. (p. 170)

- Science is like anything else, Elizabeth said. Some are better at it than others. (p. 171)

- He liked the idea of television—the way it promised people an escape from daily life. That's why he'd chosen it—because who didn't want to escape? He did. (p. 182)

  - But as the years wore on, he began to feel like he was the prisoner permanently assigned to digging the escape tunnel. At the end of the day, as the other prisoners scrambled over him to freedom, he stayed behind with the spoon.

- Humans need reassurance. They need to know others survived the hard times. And unlike other species, which do a better job of learning from their mistakes, humans require constant threats and reminders (to be nice). (p. 194)

  - You know how we say, 'People never learn?' It's because they never do. But religious texts try to keep them on track.

* . . . People need to believe in something bigger than themselves.

* "Why?" Calvin pressed. "What's wrong with believing in ourselves?"

* Anyway, if stories must be used, why not rely on a fable or fairy tale? . . . The stories were short, memorable, and covered all the bases of love, pride, folly, and forgiveness. Their rules were bite-sized: Don't be a jerk. Don't hurt other people or animals. Share what you have with others less fortunate. In other words, be nice.

• He went on to remind her he was a producer. . . . "KCTV," he said proudly, even though he wasn't. (p.196)

* [We say things that we're not proud of. Things that other people think are worthy and proud-worthy.]

• Cooking is chemistry. And chemistry is life. Your ability to change everything—including yourself—starts here. (p. 225)

* Take risks. Don't be afraid to experiment.

• She wanted to think there was some ironclad bond that connected her to them for life, but that's not how it worked. Families required constant maintenance. (p. 234)

• People needed constant reassurance that things were okay or were going to be okay instead of the more obvious reality that things were bad and were only going to get worse. (p. 243)

• Some things are private. It's not a secret; it's just that you don't know me well enough to tell me. But a secret is something we keep because there's a chance that if someone knew our secret, they would use it against us or make us feel bad. Secrets usually involve things we're ashamed of. (p. 245)

* "Do you keep secrets?" "Yes," he admitted. "How about you?" "Me too," she said.

* "I'm pretty sure everyone does," he said. "Especially the people who say they don't. There's no way you go through life without being embarrassed or ashamed about something."

- They both talk about their lineage as if they have a pedigree, but they don't. Your relatives can't make you important or smart. They can't make you *you*. (p. 245)

  - "What makes me *me*, then?" "What you choose to do. How you live your life."

- Because quite often the past belongs only in the past. Because the past is the only place it makes sense. (p. 246)

- Don't let the public tell your story for you, Miss Zott. They have a way of twisting the truth. (p. 328)

- If there's a truism in journalism, it's this: it's only when the reporter stops asking that the subject starts telling. (p. 328)

- I think [religion] lets us off the hook. I think it teaches us that nothing is really our fault; that something or someone else is pulling the strings; that ultimately, we're not to blame for the way things are; that to improve things, we should pray. But the truth is, we are very much responsible for the badness in the world. And we have the power to fix it. (p. 331)

  - I'm speaking of fixing *us*—our mistakes. Nature works on a higher intellectual plane.

- "Your mom is very famous." "Because of *Life*," the child said, hanging her head. "No," Frask said firmly. "In spite of it." (p. 347)

  - "And your mother," she continued for the first time without jealousy, "was completely in love with him."

- . . . The hard part wasn't returning to school, but rather having the courage to do so. (p. 360)

- Chemistry is change. Whenever you start doubting yourself, whenever you feel afraid, just remember. Courage is the root of change— and change is what we're chemically designed to do. So when you wake up tomorrow, make this pledge. No more holding yourself back. No more subscribing to others' opinions of what you can and cannot achieve. And no more allowing anyone to pigeonhole you. . . . Do not allow your talents to lie dormant, ladies. Design your own future. When you go home today, ask yourself what *you* will change. And then get started. (p. 360)

- A moment for yourself . . . Use that moment to reconnect with my own needs, to identify my true direction, to recommit. (p. 361)

- Madeline had once said Wakely believed some things needed to stay in the past because the past was the only place they made sense. (p. 384)

Notes

Introduction

xiii **Entrepreneurial Investment Decisions**: Laura Huang, "A Theory of Investor Gut Feel: A Test of the Impact of Gut Feel on Entrepreneurial Investment Decisions" (PhD diss., University of California, Irvine, 2012), https://www.proquest.com/dissertations-theses/theory-investor-gut-feel-test-impact-on/docview/1277650039/se-2.

xvii **screamed "bad investment"**: Dan Blystone, "The History of Uber," *Investopedia*, August 8, 2024, https://www.investopedia.com/articles/personal-finance/111015/story-uber.asp.

xvii **changes and disruption**: Out of every ten start-ups, about three or four fail completely, another three or four hobble slowly to mediocrity, and only one or two produce substantial returns. In this way, investor gut feel was not for looking at investments at a granular, deal-by-deal basis. It helped them evaluate the extremes—which deals might be the extraordinarily profitable investments within a larger set of potential investments.

xix **raise their children, rock stars**: Both literal and figurative.

xx **Adversity into Advantage**: Laura Huang, *Edge: Turning Adversity into Advantage* (Portfolio, 2020).

1: Intuition Is a Process, Gut Feel an Outcome

3 **created by Tim Berners-Lee**: Richard MacManus, "1990: Programming the World Wide Web," *Web Development History*, November 1, 2021, https://webdevelopmenthistory.com/1990-programming-the-world-wide-web.

3 **information, Ethan Zuckerman:** One of the first successful dot com companies. Ethan Zuckerman, "The Internet's Original Sin," *The Atlantic*, August 14, 2014, https://www.theatlantic.com/technology /archive/2014/08/advertising-is-the-internets-original-sin/376041.

4 **complaints from advertisers:** Adrienne LaFrance, "The First Pop-Up Ad," *The Atlantic*, August 14, 2024, https://www.theatlantic.com /technology/archive/2014/08/the-first-pop-up-ad/376053.

4 **this was *the* solution:** Ethan Zuckerman, "'We've Lost 10 Years of Innovation. This Decade Has Been Boring for the Web,'" interview with Noah Kulwin, *Intelligencer*, April 23, 2018, https://nymag.com /intelligencer/2018/04/ethan-zuckerman-inventor-of-pop-up-ad -interview.html.

4 **"content," Zuckerman explained:** LaFrance, "The First Pop-Up Ad."

5 **banner ad click-through rates:** LaFrance, "The First-Ever Banner Ad on the Web," *The Atlantic*, April 21, 2017, https://www.theatlantic.com /technology/archive/2017/04/the-first-ever-banner-ad-on-the-web /523728/.

5 **tangible results for their businesses:** Stuart Elliott, "Banner Ads on Internet Attract Users," *New York Times*, December 3, 1996, https:// www.nytimes.com/1996/12/03/business/banner-ads-on-internet -attract-users.html.

5 **campaigns across multiple websites:** Kathryn Browning, "Evolution of the Pop-Up: From Annoyance to Necessity," Justuno, November 8, 2023, https://www.justuno.com/blog/evolution-of-the-pop-up/.

5 **audience in hyper-targeted ways:** Paul Williams Short, "Should Marketers Use Pop-Up Forms? A Comprehensive Analysis," Smallbizclub, March 12, 2024, https://smallbizclub.com/sales-and-marketing /should-marketers-use-pop-up-forms-a-comprehensive-analysis/.

5 **based on cost per impression:** Will Kenton, "Cost per Thousand (CPM) Definition and Its Role in Marketing," Investopedia, August 26, 2024, https://www.investopedia.com/terms/c/cpm.asp.

5 **"the most hated advertising technique":** Therese Fessenden, "The Most Hated Online Advertising Techniques," NNGroup, June 4, 2017, https://www.nngroup.com/articles/most-hated-advertising-techniques/.

5 **"the internet's original sin":** Zuckerman, "The Internet's Original Sin."

5 **Zuckerman has even apologized:** Zuckerman, "The Internet's Original Sin."

6 **Gladwell would describe:** Malcolm Gladwell, *Blink: The Power of Thinking Without Thinking* (Back Bay Books, 2005): 3–17.

6 **claimed in *Thinking, Fast and Slow*:** Daniel Kahneman, *Thinking, Fast and Slow* (Farrar, Straus and Giroux, 2013).

7 **"insights and judgments":** Judith Orloff, *The Power of Intuition* (Hay House, 2005).

7 **"reveal its insights":** Brené Brown, *Daring Greatly* (Avery, 2012).

8 **gut feel the response (to this):** Gerd Gigerenzer, *Gut Feelings: The Intelligence of the Unconscious* (Penguin, 2007).

8 **foundational scholars of emotional intelligence:** Daniel Goleman, *The Brain and Emotional Intelligence: New Insights* (More Than Sound, 2011), https://impactconnect.com.ng/wp-content/uploads/2023/06/The _Brain_and_Emotional_Intelligence-Daniel_Goleman.pdf.

8 **bodily signals and somatic cues:** Peter Salovey and John Mayer, "Emotional Intelligence," *Imagination, Cognition and Personality* 9, no. 3 (1990): 185–211, https://doi.org/10.2190/DUGG-P24E-52WK -6CDG.

8 **instance of "Moneyball":** Michael Lewis, *Moneyball: The Art of Winning an Unfair Game* (W. W. Norton, 2003); Bennett Miller, director, *Moneyball*, Columbia Pictures, 2011.

9 **amalgam of data and experience:** David De Cremer and Garry Kasparov, "AI Should Augment Human Intelligence, Not Replace It," *Harvard Business Review*, March 18, 2021, https://www.daviddecremer .com/wp-content/uploads/HBR2021_AI-Should-Augment-Human -Intelligence-Not-Replace-It.pdf.

9 **"countermoves and outcomes":** Mike Cassidy, "Centaur Chess Shows Power of Teaming Human and Machine," *HuffPost*, December 30, 2014, https://www.huffpost.com/entry/centaur-chess-shows-power_b _6383606#.

9 **"machine + inferior process":** De Cremer and Kasparov, "AI Should Augment Human Intelligence, Not Replace It."

2: Gut Feel Is Not Easily Heard

15 **finds out she's pregnant:** Kevin Bright, director, *Friends*, season 8, episode 1, "The One After 'I Do,'" directed by Kevin Bright, NBC, September 2001, https://tvshowtranscripts.ourboard.org/viewtopic.php ?f=845&t=31537.

3: Gut Feel Is Sensed in Three Ways

23 **described his Eureka moment:** Jim Colgan and Lisa Chow, "How Twitter Was Nearly Called Twitch: Twitter Co-Founder Jack Dorsey on Coming Up with a Name," *WNYC News*, July 18, 2011, https://www .wnyc.org/story/146115-twitter-co-founder-jack-dorsey-how-his -company-was-nearly-called-twitch/.

4: Gut Feel Doesn't Lie

33 **wholesalers in the United States:** "Rick Cohen & Family," *Forbes*, September 17, 2024, https://www.forbes.com/profile/rick-cohen/.

34 **grocery distribution industry:** "About," C&S Wholesale Grocers, https://www.cswg.com/about/.

37 **C&S moved more cases:** Thomas J. DeLong, Tejal Mody, and David Ager, "C&S Wholesale Grocers: Self-Managed Teams," Harvard Business School Case 404-025, August 2003, https://www.hbs.edu /faculty/Pages/item.aspx?num=30252.

38 **first trucks to arrive:** "Hope: It's What We Bring to the Table," C&S Wholesale Grocers, C&S Community Involvement Report, 2006, https://www.cswg.com/wp-content/uploads/2020/08/CS-2006-CIR.pdf.

39 **federal government aid trucks:** "100 Years: Nourishing Communities Since 2018," C&S Wholesale Grocers, C&S Community Involvement Report, 2018, https://www.cswg.com/wp-content/uploads/2020/08 /CS-2018-CIR.pdf.

39 **fifteen thousand employees:** "C&S Wholesale Grocers," *Forbes*, September 17, 2024, https://www.forbes.com/companies/cs-wholesale-grocers/.

39 **eighth-largest privately held company:** "C&S Wholesale Grocers," *Forbes*.

39 **worth of $12.7 billion:** "Rick Cohen & Family," *Forbes*.

40 **research that biases exist:** Amos Tversky and Daniel Kahneman, "Judgment Under Uncertainty: Heuristics and Biases," *Science* 185, no. 4157 (1974): 1124–31, https://doi.org/10.1126/science.185.4157.1124.

41 **four domains represent:** Dave Snowden, "The Evolution of Cynefin Over a Decade," The Cynefin Company, February 7, 2010, https:// thecynefin.co/the-evolution-of-cynefin-over-a-decade/?srsltid =AfmBOopW8H3lYo6jy720ZVRj1MSHGm43DqVVzWAEbMR -qwOQiif4fyx6.

41 **word for *habitat*:** "Cynefin and Its Welsh Roots," The Cynefin Company, October 2020, https://thecynefin.co/library/cynefin21 -cynefin-and-its-welsh-roots/.

44 **know we don't know:** Donald Rumsfeld and Richard Myers, Department of Defense News Briefing, February 12, 2002, https://web.archive .org/web/20160406235718/http://archive.defense.gov/Transcripts /Transcript.aspx?TranscriptID=2636.

48 **"new style of music":** Taylor Swift, "1989 [Liner Notes]," Genius, October 27, 2014, https://genius.com/Taylor-swift-1989-liner-notes -annotated.

48 **"follow this gut feeling":** Taylor Swift, "1989 [Liner Notes]."

48 **"wanted to make it":** Brendan Kelly, "Taylor Swift Steps Away From Her Country Roots With 1989," *Montreal Gazette*, October 25, 2014, https://montrealgazette.com/entertainment/music/taylor-swift-steps -away-from-her-country-roots-with-1989.

48 **make a clean break:** Alan Light, "Billboard Woman of the Year Taylor Swift on Writing Her Own Rules, Not Becoming a Cliche and the Hurdle of Going Pop," *Billboard*, December 5, 2014, https://www .billboard.com/music/awards/billboard-woman-of-the-year-taylor -swift-on-writing-her-6363514/.

50 **confound decision makers:** Peter H. Bloch, Frédéric F. Brunel, and Todd J. Arnold, "Individual Differences in the Centrality of Visual Product Aesthetics: Concept and Measurement," *Journal of Consumer Research* 29, no. 4 (2003): 551–65, https://doi.org/10.1086 /346250.

50 **situational normality:** Harmony (White, 1996); Jonas Löwgren, "Pliability as an Experiential Quality: Exploring the Aesthetics of Interaction Design," *Artifact* 1, no. 2 (2007): 85–95, http://dx.doi.org /10.1080/17493460600976165; musicality (Linstead, 2006); Rafael Ramírez, "The Aesthetics of Cooperation," *European Management Review* 2, no. 1 (2005): 28–35, https://doi.org/10.1057/palgrave.emr .1500028; Mike Baer et al., "Trusting the 'Look and Feel': Situational Normality, Situational Aesthetics, and the Perceived Trustworthiness of Organizations," *Academy of Management Journal* 61, no. 5 (2017): 1718–40, https://doi.org/10.5465/amj.2016.0248.

5: Gut Feel Compels Action (and Re-Action)

53 **output of platinum and diamonds:** Cynthia Carroll, "The CEO of Anglo American on Getting Serious About Safety," *Harvard Business Review*, June 2012, https://hbr.org/2012/06/the-ceo-of-anglo-american-on-getting-serious-about-safety.

53 **share of De Beers:** "Diamonds," Anglo American, accessed September 21, 2024, https://www.angloamerican.com/products/diamonds.

53 **ninety-five thousand permanent employees:** "Why Anglo American," Anglo American, accessed September 21, 2024, https://www.angloamerican.com/careers/why-anglo-american.

53 **thirty thousand contract employees:** "At a Glance," Anglo American, accessed September 21, 2024, https://www.angloamericanplatinum.com/about-us/at-a-glance.

53 **first female chief executive:** Timmons, "Tradition-Breaking Choice to Be Chief of Mining Giant."

53 **executive of Anglo American:** Heather Timmons, "Tradition-Breaking Choice to Be Chief of Mining Giant," *New York Times*, October 25, 2006, https://www.nytimes.com/2006/10/25/business/worldbusiness/25mine.html.

53 **"another fatality":** Carroll, "The CEO of Anglo American on Getting Serious About Safety."

55 **"killing people":** Gautam Mukunda, "'We Thought She Was Crazy': Why Values Guide You in a Crisis," *Forbes*, June 25, 2020, https://www.forbes.com/sites/gautammukunda/2020/06/25/we-thought-she-was-crazy-why-values-guide-you-in-a-crisis/.

55 **enabled them to voice their concerns:** Gautam Mukunda, Lisa Mazzanti, and Aldo Sesia, "Cynthia Carroll at Anglo American (A)," Harvard Business School Case 414-019, October 2013, https://www.hbs.edu/faculty/Pages/item.aspx?num=45820.

56 **weeks before the mines reopened:** Carroll, "The CEO of Anglo American on Getting Serious about Safety."

56 **10 Fatal Risk Standards:** "Anglo American Fatal Risk Standards," Anglo American, May 2008, https://www.angloamerican.com.au/-/media/Files/A/Anglo-American-Australia-V2/Attachments/content/AFRS.pdf.

56 **Tripartite Safety Summit:** "Transforming the Way Anglo
    American Does Business," Anglo American, August 24, 2009,
    https://www.angloamerican.com/media/press-releases/archive/2009
    /2009-08-24.

56 **set of Guiding Values:** "Making a Difference: Report to Society 2008,"
    Anglo American, March 2009, https://www.angloamerican.com
    /~/media/Files/A/Anglo-American-Group-v5/PLC/investors/annual
    -reporting/2009/rts-08-final.pdf.

56 **Management Programme:** "Anglo American Launches Innovative
    Safety Risk Management Programme Across the Mining Industry,"
    Anglo American, May 17, 2010, https://www.angloamerican.com/media
    /press-releases/archive/2010/safety_risk_management.

57 **stepped down in April 2013:** Gautam Mukunda, Lisa Mazzanti, and
    Aldo Sesia, "Cynthia Carroll at Anglo American (A)."

59 **Hill once conducted an analysis:** Napoleon Hill, *Think and Grow Rich*
    (The Ralston Society, 1937).

61 **Magic Eye posters:** Liz Stinson, "The Hidden History of Magic Eye,
    the Optical Illusion That Briefly Took Over the World," AIGA Eye
    on Design, July 1, 2022, https://eyeondesign.aiga.org/the-hidden
    -history-of-magic-eye-the-optical-illusion-that-briefly-took-over-the
    -world/.

62 **Food for all:** "About Us," Brigaid, accessed September 21, 2024, https://
    www.chefsbrigaid.com/about.

65 **per my dissertation:** Huang, "A Theory of Investor Gut Feel:
    A Test of the Impact of Gut Feel on Entrepreneurial Investment
    Decisions."

66 **generate expense reports:** "About," TravelBank, accessed September 21,
    2024, https://travelbank.com/about/.

66 **Lai, one of the managing directors:** "Carey Lai: Founding
    Managing Director," Conductive, accessed September 21, 2024,
    https://conductive.vc/.

67 **acquired by US Bancorp:** Mark Reilly, "U.S. Bancorp Buys Travelbank,
    Fintech Backed by Will Smith," *Minneapolis/St. Paul Business Journal*,
    November 16, 2021, https://www.bizjournals.com/twincities/news
    /2021/11/16/u-s-bancorp-buys-travelbank.html.

6: Perceptible: How Do I Engage My Intuition?

71 *The Stone Journey*: Lei Mingwei, *The Stone Journey*, 2010, mixed media installation, glacial stone, bronze, and wood, eleven sets, 10.5 x 50 x 15 cm each, https://www.leemingwei.com/.

7: Personified: How Do I Describe Myself?

85 the wall telepathically": Eliza Thompson, "Ariana Grande and Mac Miller Are Super-Flirty Neighbors in Their New Video," *Cosmopolitan*, December 13, 2016, https://www.cosmopolitan.com/entertainment/music/a8495174/ariana-grande-mac-miller-video/.

85 "obvious to anyone": Dalai Lama (@dalailama), "Whether or not we follow any particular spiritual tradition, the benefits of love and kindness are obvious to anyone," X, October 10, 2011, 5:28 a.m., https://x.com/DalaiLama/status/123329118124253184.

85 called *forward flow*: Kurt Gray, Stephen Anderson, Eric Evan Chen, John Michael Kelly, Michael S. Christian, John Patrick, Laura Huang, Yoed N. Kenett, and Kevin Lewis, "'Forward Flow': A New Measure to Quantify Free Thought and Predict Creativity," *American Psychologist* 74, no. 5 (2019): 539–54, https://doi.org/10.1037/amp0000391.

90 Myers-Briggs Type Indicator: "Myers-Briggs Overview," Myers & Briggs Foundation, accessed September 21, 2024, https://www.myersbriggs.org/my-mbti-personality-type/myers-briggs-overview/.

90 The Enneagram: "How the Enneagram System Works," The Enneagram Institute, accessed September 21, 2024, https://www.enneagraminstitute.com/how-the-enneagram-system-works/.

90 The Big Five model: Annabelle G. Y. Lim, "Big Five Personality Traits: The 5-Factor Model of Personality," *Simply Psychology*, December 20, 2023, https://www.simplypsychology.org/big-five-personality.html.

92 Altucher writes ten ideas: James Altucher, "The Ultimate Guide for Becoming an Idea Machine," *James Altucher Blog*, accessed September 21, 2024, https://archive.jamesaltucher.com/blog/the-ultimate-guide-for-becoming-an-idea-machine/.

93 Home Run Derby: Juan Toribio, "Vlad Jr. Sets Records in Stunning Derby Display," MLB.com, July 9, 2019, https://www.mlb.com/news/vladimir-guerrero-jr-2019-mlb-home-run-derby.

93 **beat a number of other heavy hitters:** "Alonso Outslugs Vlad Jr. to Win Home Run Derby," *ESPN*, July 8, 2019, https://www.espn.com/mlb /story/_/id/27150117/alonso-outslugs-vlad-jr-win-home-run-derby.

94 **using a Dove Tail Bat:** Renee Cordes, "Maine-Made Baseball Bat to Star in Major League Home Run Derby," *Mainebiz*, July 16, 2022, https://www.mainebiz.biz/article/maine-made-baseball-bat-to-star-in -major-league-home-run-derby.

95 **Australia, and Japan:** "Dove Tail Bats, LLC," CEI Stories, Coastal Enterprises, Inc., January 9, 2017, https://www.ceimaine.org/about/cei -stories/dove-tail-bats-llc/.

95 **thirty thousand baseball bats:** "Dove Tail Bats Unveils Big League Technology for Baseball," Dove Tail Bats, May 10, 2023, https:// dovetailbat.com/blogs/news/dove-tail-bats-unveils-big-league -technology-for-baseball?srsltid=AfmBOorwc-zUBXjF7GAz7Hvy ZWvNQJojMsyo9RFSHJqKEN1YXknWKwIY.

95 **inducted in baseball's Hall of Fame:** "Dove Tail Bats Unveils Big League Technology for Baseball," Dove Tail Bats.

8: Embodied: Where Do I Feel That?

103 **because of trauma:** Research about embodied trauma . . . Gabor Mate and Bessel van der Kolk's ideas.

103 **"since World War II":** Warren Bennis, *Still Surprised: A Memoir of a Life in Leadership* (San Francisco, CA: Jossey-Bass, 2010): 35.

104 **advisor to four US presidents:** "Warren Bennis (1925–2014)," University of Southern California, https://ahf.usc.edu/usc-awards/bennis -scholars/about-warren-bennis/.

104 **"timeless Renaissance man":** Ying Wang, "Positively Pioneering," *Harvard Crimson*, June 7, 2006, https://www.thecrimson.com/article /2006/6/7/positively-pioneering-professor-of-psychology-philip/.

106 **context in which an interaction:** Francisco Varela, Evan Thompson, and Eleanor Rosch, "The Embodied Mind: Cognitive Science and Human Experience."

106 **grounded in bodily experiences:** George Lakoff and Mark Johnson, *Metaphors We Live By* (University of Chicago Press, 1980).

106 **grounded in our bodily experiences:** John Dewey, "The Theory of Emotion. 2. The Significance of Emotions," *Psychological Review* 2 (1895): 13–32, https://brocku.ca/MeadProject/Dewey/Dewey_1895.html.

9: Emotional: How Do I Feel?

111 **two-dimensional plane:** Jonathan Posner, James A. Russell, and Bradley S. Peterson, "The Circumplex Model of Affect: An Integrative Approach to Affective Neuroscience, Cognitive Development, and Psychopathology," *Development and Psychopathology* 17, no. 3 (2005): 715–34, https://doi .org/10.1017/S0954579405050340.

111 **arousal, and dominance:** Albert Mehrabian, *Basic Dimensions for a General Psychological Theory: Implications for Personality, Social, Environmental, and Developmental Studies* (Oelgeschlager, Gunn & Hain, 1980).

112 **and negative affect:** David Watson, Lee Anna Clark, and Auke Tellegen, "Development and Validation of Brief Measures of Positive and Negative Affect: The PANAS Scales," *Journal of Personality and Social Psychology* 54, no. 6 (1988): 1063–70, https://doi.org/10.1037 /0022-3514.54.6.1063.

10: Cognitive: How Do I Construct Concepts?

124 **can't tell time:** "1 in 6 People Can't Tell the Time, According to Research," ITVX, March 16, 2023, https://www.itv.com/thismorning /articles/1-in-6-people-cant-tell-the-time-according-to-research.

125 **Schemas are generalized:** Frederic C. Bartlett, *Remembering: A Study in Experimental and Social Psychology* (Cambridge University Press, 1932); Roger C. Schank and Robert P. Abelson, "Scripts, Plans and Knowledge," International Joint Conference on Artificial Intelligence (1975); David E. Rumelhart, "Schemata: The Building Blocks of Cognition," in Rand J. Spiro, Bertram C. Bruce, and William F. Brewer, eds., *Theoretical Issues in Reading Comprehension: Perspectives From Cognitive Psychology, Linguistics, Artificial Intelligence, and Education* (Erlbaum, 1980).

126 **models are more specific:** Philip Nicholas Johnson-Laird, "Mental Models in Cognitive Science," *Cognitive Science* 4, no. 1 (1980): 71–115, https://doi.org/10.1016/S0364-0213(81)80005-5; Johnson-Laird, *Mental Models: Towards a Cognitive Science of Language, Inference, and Consciousness* (Harvard University Press, 1983); Teun A. van Dijk and Walter Kinsch, *Strategies of Discourse Composition* (Academic Press, 1983); Rolf A. Zwaan and Gabriel A. Radvansky, "Situational Models in Language Comprehension and Memory," *Psychological Bulletin* 123, no. 2 (1998): 162–85, https://doi.org/10.1037/0033-2909.123.2.162.

130 **Musk invested his own money:** Shikhar Ghosh and Sarah Mehta, "Elon Musk: Balancing Purpose and Risk," Harvard Business School Case 817-040, October 2016, https://www.hbs.edu/faculty/Pages/item.aspx ?num=51769.

130 **launched Amazon from his garage:** Peter Westberg, "Jeff Bezos: Building an Empire from A to Z," *Quartr*, October 24, 2023, https://quartr.com /insights/business-philosophy/jeff-bezos-building-an-empire-from-a-to-z.

130 **contribute to her vast wealth:** David Olusegun, "How Oprah Winfrey Became the World's First and Richest Black Woman Billionaire," *Creators Blueprint*, June 5, 2023, https://www.creatorsblueprint.co/p /how-oprah-winfrey-became-the-worlds.

131 **gave away the company:** David Gelles, "Billionaire No More: Patagonia Founder Gives Away the Company," *New York Times*, September 14, 2022, https://www.nytimes.com/2022/09/14/climate/patagonia-climate -philanthropy-chouinard.html.

131 **collapsed in 2001:** John Schwartz and Richard A. Oppel Jr., "ENRON'S COLLAPSE: THE CHIEF EXECUTIVE; Foundation Gives Way on Chief's Big Dream," *New York Times*, November 29, 2001, https:// www.nytimes.com/2001/11/29/business/enron-s-collapse-the-chief -executive-foundation-gives-way-on-chief-s-big-dream.html.

131 **mismanaged his company:** Gabriel Sherman, "'You Don't Bring Bad News to the Cult Leader': Inside the Fall of WeWork," *Vanity Fair*, November 21, 2019, https://www.vanityfair.com/news/2019/11/inside -the-fall-of-wework.

11: What Does *Your* Eureka, Spidey Sense, or Jolt Feel Like?

150 *The Alchemist* **by Paulo Coelho:** Paulo Coelho, *The Alchemist* (HarperCollins, English translation, 1993).

151 **Quaker, and the US Postal Service):** Gary Hoover, "The Unsung Story of the Greatest Industrial Designer," Archbridge Institute, October 30, 2019, https://www.archbridgeinstitute.org/the-unsung-story-of-the -greatest-industrial-designer/.

152 **"make it surprising":** Derek Thompson, "The Four-Letter Code to Sell Just About Anything," *The Atlantic*, January/February 2017, https:// www.theatlantic.com/magazine/archive/2017/01/what-makes-things -cool/508772/.

152 **Öllinger, who have studied:** Guenther Knoblich and Michael Öllinger, "The Eureka Moment," *Scientific American Mind* 17, no. 5 (2006): 38–43, http://dx.doi.org/10.1038/scientificamericanmind1006-38.

152 **Sprugnoli and colleagues have found:** Giulia Sprugnoli, Simone Rossi, Alexandra Emmendorfer, Alessandro Rossi, Sook-Lei Liew, Elisa Tatti, Giorgio di Lorenzo, Alvaro Pascual-Leone, and Emiliano Santarnecci, "Neural Correlates of *Eureka* Moment," *Intelligence* 62 (2017): 99–118, https://doi.org/10.1016/j.intell.2017.03.004.

155 **railway lines in Japan:** Yukako, "TESSEI: The 7 Minute Miracle of the Bullet Train Cleaning Crew," Harvard Business School Digital Initiative, Technology and Operations Management MBA Perspectives, December 9, 2015, https://d3.harvard.edu/platform-rctom/submission /tessei-the-7-minute-miracle-of-the-bullet-train-cleaning-crew/.

155 **Tessei crew is tasked:** Danielle Demetriou, "High-Speed Cleaning Teams Behind Japan's High-Speed Bullet Trains," *Telegraph*, June 23, 2015, https://www.telegraph.co.uk/news/worldnews/asia/japan/11692858 /High-speed-cleaning-teams-behind-Japans-high-speed-bullet-trains.html.

12: Focused Abstraction

161 **novel, *The Sun Also Rises*:** Ernest Hemingway, *The Sun Also Rises* (Charles Scribner's Sons, 1926).

162 **Spin Pop, was a lollipop:** Knowledge at Wharton Staff, "Toys and Spinning Brushes: How John Osher Found His Way to Profits," *Knowledge at Wharton*, November 19, 2003, https://knowledge.wharton .upenn.edu/article/toys-and-spinning-brushes-how-john-osher-found-his -way-to-profits/.

162 **he sold Spin Pop:** Knowledge at Wharton Staff, "Toys and Spinning Brushes."

166 **"light bulb goes on":** Henry Rollins, "Interview with Henry Rollins: Punk Rock World Traveler," interview with Jim Benning, *World Hum*, November 2, 2011, http://www.worldhum.com/features/travel-interviews /interview-with-henry-rollins-punk-rock-travel-20111101/.

13: Prompted Action

170 **"experience on a daily basis":** Miranda Levingston, "UP5 Preview— Amanda Phingbodhipakkiya: The Neuroscientist-Artist Fighting Anti-

Asian Racism," *UP Magazine*, https://upmag.com/amanda
-phingbodhipakkiya/.

170 **commissioned mural:** *State Magazine*, "Embassy Bangkok Unveils
Women's Empowerment Mural," January 2023, https://statemag.state
.gov/2023/01/0123ib02/.

170 **"can I force them":** *Allgemeine musikalische Zeitung*, 17:34 (August 23,
1815), cols. 561–66; trans. *Harmonicon* 35 (November 1825): 198.

170 **"smarter than I was":** Paul Dirac, quoted in Viktor Dörfler and Fran
Ackermann, "Understanding Intuition: The Case for Two Forms of
Intuition," *Management Learning* 43, no. 5 (2012): 545–64.

171 **said, "Ew, gross!":** Olivia B. Waxman, "The Story Behind TIME's
Cover on Anti-Asian Violence and Hate Crimes," *TIME*, March 18,
2021, https://time.com/5947622/time-cover-anti-asian-american
-violence-atlanta-shooting/.

171 *Believe in Our City*: Amanda Phingbodhipakkiya, "I Still Believe in
Our City," Art installation, https://www.istillbelieve.nyc/.

171 **"unsung or the unseen":** Waxman, "The Story Behind TIME's Cover
on Anti-Asian Violence and Hate Crimes."

172 **March 2021 issue:** Waxman, "The Story Behind TIME's Cover on
Anti- Asian Violence and Hate Crimes."

174 **traveled to Thailand:** "Weaving Our Stories," US Embassy and
Consulate in Thailand, accessed September 21, 2024, https://th
.usembassy.gov/weaving-our-stories/.

175 **"biases and goals?":** Ashton Jackson, "Ray Dalio Says This One Question
Will Help You Uncover Someone's True Motives: 'This Applies to
Everything,'" CNBC, October 19, 2023, https://www.cnbc.com/2023
/10/19/ray-dalio-shares-his-no-1-rule-to-identify-your-true-friends
-.html.

175 **"things they want":** Ashton Jackson, "Ray Dalio Says This One
Question Will Help You Uncover Someone's True Motives."

178 **often sends signals:** Kenna D. S. Lehmann, Brian W. Goldman,
Ian Dworkin, David M. Bryson, and Aaron P. Wagner, "From
Cues to Signals: Evolution of Interspecific Communication via
Aposematism and Mimicry in a Predator-Prey System," *PLOS
ONE* 9, no. 3 (2014): e91783, https://doi.org/10.1371/journal
.pone.0091783.

179 **provides a cue:** Mark E. Laidre and Rufus A. Johnstone, "Animal Signals," *Current Biology* 23, no. 18, (2013): R829–33, https://doi.org /10.1016/j.cub.2013.07.070.

14: The Relevance of Experience

183 **repeated twenty times?:** Andrew Hargadon, quoted in Jeffrey Pfeffer, "Teaching Power in Ways that Influence Students' Career Success: Some Fundamental Ideas," Stanford University, December 2019, https://jeffreypfeffer.com/wp-content/uploads/2019/12/SSRN -id3493406.pdf.

183 **new CEO of JCPenney:** Andrew Chang, "J.C. Penney Names Apple's Ron Johnson as Its New CEO," *Los Angeles Times*, June 15, 2011, https://www.latimes.com/business/la-xpm-2011-jun-15-la-fi-0615 -jcpenney-ceo-20110615-story.html.

184 **or "Tar-zhay":** Andria Cheng, "Ron Johnson Made Apple Stores the Envy of Retail and Target Hip, But This Startup May Be His Crowning Achievement," *Forbes*, January 17, 2020, https://www.forbes.com/sites /andriacheng/2020/01/17/he-made-apple-stores-envy-of-retail-and -target-hip-but-his-biggest-career-chapter-may-be-just-starting/.

184 **created the Apple store experience:** Andria Cheng, "Ron Johnson Made Apple Stores the Envy of Retail and Target Hip, But This Startup May Be His Crowning Achievement."

184 **he was fired:** Steve Schaefer, "Ron Johnson Out at J.C. Penney, Replaced by Former Chief Mike Ullman," *Forbes*, April 8, 2013, https:// www.forbes.com/sites/steveschaefer/2013/04/08/ron-johnson-out-at-j-c -penney-replaced-by-former-chief-mike-ullman/.

184 **"a ridiculous one":** Voltaire, quoted in William Messer, *The Sayings of Voltaire* (Bibliomundi, 2018).

185 **Thorstein Veblen calls:** Thorstein Veblen, quoted in Herman Kahn, "The Expert and Educated Incapacity," Hudson Institute Reports, June 1, 1979, https://www.hudson.org/economics/the-expert-and-educated -incapacity.

186 **"Fair and Square" pricing strategy:** Elie Ofek and Jill Avery, "J.C. Penney's 'Fair and Square' Pricing Strategy," Harvard Business School Case 513-036, September 2012, https://www.hbs.edu/faculty/Pages /item.aspx?num=43132.

186 **significant financial losses**: Schaefer, "Ron Johnson Out at J.C. Penney,
Replaced by Former Chief Mike Ullman."
189 **"same as loving it"**: Gabrielle Zevin, *Tomorrow, and Tomorrow, and
Tomorrow* (Knopf, 2022).

15: The Value of Mistakes
192 **"one is fundamental"**: Jensen Huang, quoted in Pushkar Ranade,
"The Leadership Philosophy of Jensen Huang," *Bits and Bytes*, Substack,
October 17, 2023, https://semiconductor.substack.com/p/the-leadership
-philosophy-of-jensen.

Conclusion: Deploy Your Superpower
204 **"difficult to master"**: Nolan Bushnell, quoted in Ian Bogost, "Persuasive
Games: Familiarity, Habituation, and Catchiness," *Game Developer*,
April 2, 2009, https://www.gamedeveloper.com/design/persuasive-games
-familiarity-habituation-and-catchiness.

Index

Italicized page numbers indicate material in tables or illustrations.